MW00437465

The Secrets Known Only To The Inner Elites

Lyndon H. LaRouche, Jr.

EIR News Service, Inc. • **Washington, D.C.**

Also by the author:

So, You Wish to Learn All About Economics?

Earth's Next Fifty Years

The State of Our Union: The End of Our Delusion!

The Economics of the Noosphere

The Power of Reason 1988

Cover: adapted from original cover of *Campaigner* magazine, Vol. II, No. 3-4, May-June 1978 in which this book was first published

Amazon Print on Demand Edition

ISBN: 9781520498263

Note From The Editors

Since this book is one of the most important books ever written, great effort has been made to make the original large scale magazine-sized maps and charts intelligible in this smaller paperback format. Whenever there is a potential problem in the legibility of a chart, you will find the important information extracted in a caption below.

Black and white images of historic paintings have been replaced with public domain versions in color.

The text is the original from the May-June 1978 edition of *The Campaigner* magazine.

About The Cover

The cover features Plato and Aristotle, shown in a detail from Raphael's famous "School of Athens." Following convention based on Aristotelian myth, Raphael portrayed the two philosophers in friendly discourse, the aging Plato on the left pointing to the heavens to illustrate his stress on the role of the mind, and the younger Aristotle pointing to the earth to symbolize his preoccupation with "solid" reality. While the Campaigner rips apart this myth to detail the actual bitter battle between the Platonic and Aristotelian elites that continues to this day, it is by no means to be presumed that Raphael was unaware of the dichotomy between the two tendencies. Significantly, Raphael--a pupil of the great Neoplatonic humanist Leonardo da Vinci--has given his Plato the features of his master, Leonardo.

Contents

THE SECRETS KNOWN ONLY TO THE INNER ELITES

By Lyndon H. LaRouche Jr.

Through three millenia of recorded history to date, centered around the Mediterranean, the civilized world has been run by two, bitterly opposed elites, the one associated with the faction of Socrates and Plato, the other with the faction of Aristotle. During these thousands of years, until the developments of approximately1784-1818 in Europe, both factions' inner elites maintained in some fashion an unbroken continuity of organization and knowledge through all of the political catastrophes which afflicted each of them in various times and locales.

FOREWORD

The cleverest way, psychologically, in which to hide a secret is to divert the investigator down a tiring trail toward a false discovery. His own efforts convince him either that he has found a secret through great energy and cleverness on his own part, or, if the secret he seeks appears still but to barely elude his grasp, he values all the more his continued course of misdirection. That is the lesson which

1

can be learned from Edgar Allan Poe's fictional case of *The Purloined Letter*.

Exemplary of the follies into which presumably educated and informed people are misled in the pursuit of the snipe, are the doctrines of the "international Jewish conspiracy" and the recently more popular "international communist conspiracy." During the twentieth century, more people have been turned into dupes along those two false-trail pursuits than any competing obsessions.

The effect of that sort of misdirected search for the ultimate, global master-conspiracy is principally twofold. The dupes themselves are misled away from the secrets being hidden in this manner. Secondly, the discredit which is directed to fall upon the lured turns most others, foolishly, away from all searches for the secrets of those "inner elites" which have in fact run the world's affairs during approximately three thousand years of known history.

To illustrate the corollary aspect of the problem: during a meeting between this writer and a leading political figure of Italy, which occurred during early 1976, the latter asked: "Why is it that Ugo La Malfa always comes out on top?" The context of his question was the period of initial efforts to replace the La Malfa-preferred Moro government with an Andreotti government. In the course of most of the postwar political crises in Italy, tiny, now-aging Ugo La Malfa, spokesman for the relatively tiny Republican Party of Italy, appeared to play the tunes to which Italy subsequently danced.

The answer to that particular question is essentially:

Ugo La Malfa has been a key Italian agent-of-influence for British intelligence services all of his adult life.

This is not to suggest that British intelligence services' operatives individually are supermen. In general, such agents, including leading operatives, are a poor lot; short attention-spans, scatterbrained, without moral mooring worth mention, easily provoked into loss of personal self-control, the majority downright louts, boors. So, Ugo La Malfa himself. It is not British intelligence services viewed in the terms the presumably informed layman ordinarily thinks of an intelligence service which are relevant to the indicated problem of La Malfa. Although British networks do have, inclusively, the sort of characteristics the misinformed layman would expect-- more or less, it is not such incidentals which account for La Malfa's past successes.

The relevant key point can be abstracted fairly thus. Since the English traitors Robert Cecil and Francis Bacon around the onset of the seventeenth century, and later, more notably, from the 1660 Stuart Restoration to the present day, within and behind British intelligence regular and irregular services there is an inner circle representing the ranks of the Black Guelph families of all Europe, an oligarchy gathered around the privileges and powers of the British and Dutch monarchies.[1]   Attached to and overlapping these oligarchical families, there is a special collectivity, traditionally centered notably in Oxford, Cambridge, and Sussex universities, an inner intelligentsia of that faction, which studies the classics, thereby to gain the knowledge through which the forces associated with the British monarchy may rule the world.

Through three millennia of recorded history to date, centered around the Mediterranean, the civilized world has been run by two, bitterly opposed elites, the one associated with the faction of Socrates and Plato, the other with the faction of Aristotle. During these thousands of years, until the developments of approximately 1784-1818 in Europe, both factions' inner elites maintained in some fashion an unbroken continuity of organization and knowledge through all of the political catastrophes which afflicted each of them in various times and locales.

It was the elite associated with the Platonic (or, Neoplatonic) faction which organized the American Revolution and established the United States as a democratic constitutional republic. During the early eighteenth century, in circumstances associated with Marlborough's campaign and the Mississippi and South-Sea bubbles plots, the continuity of the Platonic faction was first administered a broad, temporary defeat with some lasting effects, and was shattered later as a world force through the events of 1784-1818.

In the aftermath of the 1815 Treaty of Vienna, the shattering of the power of the Platonic elite in Europe meant in large measure both a scattering of the main forces of that faction, and an associated, increasing loss of the "secret knowledge" through which the Platonic inner elite had formerly developed and exercised its factional power. From that time to the present period, the inner circles of the Aristotelian (or, more exactly, "neo-Aristotelian") faction have been hegemonic increasingly in ordering world affairs. Although humanist (Platonic) factional forces have continued in existence and are represented among political and related elites today, the Platonic elite has lost connection to the body of knowledge upon which its former power depended.

The person who posed the question cited is exemplary of this problem. He is not only a Christian humanist and a member of the ruling political elite, but a man of unusual personal character as well as political skills and power. Yet, with the considerable knowledge available to him, he did not know the answer to the question. Any member of the Platonic elite in command of the "secret knowledge" of that tradition would have known the answer immediately.

The principal function of this report is to summarily, but systematically identify the "secret knowledge" of the Platonic inner elite. That includes the Platonic's knowledge of the secrets of the enemy, Aristotelian elite.

Although the objective of this writer and his associates is to end the ages-long division between elites and the credulous, myth-ridden masses, this can not be accomplished usefully by bringing the elite down to the ignorance of the masses. The masses must be brought up out of mythology's grip, to attain the qualities of the Platonic elite. That accomplishment is impossible without the leading role of a reconstituted Platonic elite--education is impossible without the educators.

Such a transformation of the mass of plebeians is the work of years, even under favorable circumstances. At this moment of writing, it would be criminal folly to propose to wait years before bringing the Platonic faction back into a leading position in the government of society.

The Dutch humanist Rembrandt drew on classical subject matter to depict the 17th century conspiracy of Anglo-Dutch monetarists. The painting is his 1662 "Oath of Julius Civilis," who was the leader of the revolt of the Batavians--a German tribe purportedly ancestors of the Dutch--against the Romans. According to the classical historian Tacitus, the one-eyed Civilis was evil and won the Batavians' leaders' support for the revolt after luring them to a banquet in a pagan grove. In the original the pagan torchlight casts an eerie yellow-gold glow, evocative of monetarists' gold hoards.

If the neo-Aristotelian faction prevails through the present period of crises, it is more than conceivable that the human race might not survive, or, at best, that the new beginnings of civilization would have to be assembled from the shards of general thermonuclear war.

The Platonic elite in the fullness of its knowledge must be reconstituted now. That cannot occur unless the "secret knowledge" of that faction is reestablished with aid of reference to classical knowledge, classical knowledge resurrected in appropriately modern terms of reference. That indispensable articulation is the function of this report.

THE CONSPIRATORS

Yes, Adelaide, the world has been run by conspiratorial elites employing secret knowledge. In its lesser aspects, that conspiracy, has subsumed features which coincide at first impression with what you might imagine a conspiracy to be. However, if you pursue the investigation from the standpoint of your usual, misguided preconceptions of a "global conspiracy," you will only mislead yourself into another pathetic concoction of mixed facts, half-truths and fantasies, like the concoctions associated with the "international Jewish conspiracy" or "international communist conspiracy."

Global conspiracies which function succeed by establishing "controlled environments" around the minds of the credulous masses of the world. Such a controlled environment is summed up efficiently by stating that the credulous masses are ruled by mythologies, and that the elites rule such masses by creating, shaping, and manipulating the mythologies. The methods employed by Joseph Goebbels and carried further by British intelligence networks for creating and manipulating the mythologies of credulous masses through control of all or at least key portions of the press and radio and television, are the center of modern techniques to this effect.

Outside and above the foolish folk who rely upon the *Washington Post, New York Times,* London *Times,* or the popular women's magazines, and so on and so forth, there is indeed a governing elite. This elite does possess "secret knowledge." The first aspect of this special knowledge, which makes it efficiently secret, is that the elite not only know that the mythologies are mythologies, but also know that they themselves create and use those mythologies to manipulate the credulous masses.

Beyond that first broad level of division between the knowledgeable and the credulous, the secret knowledge is distinguished by the division of elites into two irreconcilable factions. Beyond the sheep-pens of the believers in mythologies, there exist two fundamentally opposed views of what to do with the world, of what direction to adopt in steering the historical movement of the human species. One elite, the humanists, the Platonic or Neoplatonic faction, is dedicated to steering the course of history away from rule through mythologies. The other, the Aristotelians and their heirs, is committed to strengthening the rule by mythology, for the purpose of establishing a permanent. "feudal-like" utopia of obedient, simple-minded folk ruled by a tenured neo-Aristotelian oligarchy.

The secret knowledge is, at first distinction, as secret as the purloined letter of the Poe tale. Once the mythologies are known to be mythologies, the primitive aspect of truth lies factually in plain sight. Once mythology is cast aside, the development of real knowledge out of such primitive truth, the development properly termed scientific progress, begins.

In the case of La Malfa, the point to be made is this.
Ugo La Malfa, like Cuccia of Mediobanca, Riccardo Lombardi of the Socialist Party of Italy, and

Amendola and Napolitano of the leadership of the Communist Party of Italy, began his career as a British intelligence services' agent under the tutelage of the same evil Benedetto Croce who mentally crippled Antonio Gramsci and many others. Together with the British intelligence services' Italian Mafia, and the British-allied "black nobility" of Italy, the networks radiating from Croce's original base at Naples University are among the principal forces that presently govern Italy from within for London. In the end, it is the Black Guelph oligarchy of Italy which is the local branch of the real rulers. The Mafia, together with such persons as La Malfa, Lombardi, and Amendola are merely the expendable mercenaries.

The central figure of the work of Croce, the key to his usefulness to his British masters, was his circle's mastery of the Italian mythologies. As scientific or scholarly work, Croce's writings on Hegel and aesthetics are infantile rubbish. However, they are not merely rubbish; they represent a model for the nonsense an ignorant, superstitious Italian will tend to swallow. In this way, Croce and his circle made themselves craftmasters of the manipulation of Italy's characteristic mythologies. They are the qualified sheepherders of the sheep of Italy, the sheep who have made up the majority of Italy's myth-ridden population.

On this account it should be readily understood that the notable folly of La Malfa's opponents is that they esteem themselves "practical politicians." In other words, they are at their best and their worst Machiavellians. As with Machiavelli in his fatal worst feature, they define the art of ruling as one of bending with the winds of prevailing mythologies--the mythologies employed by their adversaries. They seek to bend the levers of such prevailing mythology, intending so to move political processes into directions which correspond in actuality with the real interests of Italy and its people. By committing such a blunder of "practical politics"--sometimes termed "ductility"--they commit themselves to leading within the limits of the sheep-pen that La Malfa and his British masters control, the sheep-pen of the British-controlled Italian mythologies.

A popularized mythology is like a goldfish bowl. No matter how cleverly the fish chooses his direction within the bowl, he can never escape it in such a fashion. No matter how cleverly he adapts to the environment of the bowl's ,medium (e.g., popular mythologies), whoever moves the bowl moves him in a corresponding direction.

The misguided "realists," the self-esteemed "practical politicians" of Italy's humanist forces, regard it as wisdom to maintain influence and credibility in terms of popular political mythologies, to attempt to bend the internal features of enemy-controlled mythologies in the direction agreeable to the interests of the nation and its people. Those for whom La Malfa speaks control the medium within which the humanists so situate themselves. Thus, and not by any advantage of personal prowess, La Malfa has often appeared to win in most of the political crises of Italy to date.

The same political arrangement prevails in North America and throughout Western Europe to the present day. It prevails in most of the developing sector, and in a somewhat different form in Eastern Europe. Only a relative handful of persons in any nation have knowledge of the true reasons behind the policies currently at issue. The masses, together with most of the persons ordinarily considered national leaders, know only the myths, the mythologies through which their minds and wills are manipulated by others.

The institutions of ballot-democracy--massive vote-frauds momentarily overlooked--have done little to improve this on principle. What does it mean to have the power to vote, if massive vote-frauds determine the official tallies, or, if the knowledge given to the voter is predominantly a myth, and if the voter's criteria of judgment are chiefly mythological? If you, Adelaide, are a typical plebeian, you are still today largely a puppet of those elites which control the shaping and manipulation of your adopted mythologies.

THE ARISTOTELIAN ENEMIES OF MANKIND

For reasons better understood on the basis of the body of this report, the only effectively ruling elite in the capitalist sector of the world today has been the neo-Aristotelian faction's inner circles, the inner circles of a force centered in Britain. The humanist elite exists, but, with handfuls of exceptions relatively speaking--chiefly scattered exceptions--lacks the "secret knowledge" upon which its global effectiveness depends. For reasons we shall identify in due course, the present center of the power of the neo-Aristotelian or oligarchical faction, the "Persian model" faction, is the Black Guelph monarchies of Britain and Holland, the power of both monarchies consolidated under the British. So, as we account for the Black Guelph faction as a whole, we focus here upon its center, the British monarchy.

One of the most notable frauds afoot in today's credulous world is the myth of British "democracy," British "constitutional government." Britain has in fact two governments, the first a parliamentary charade for the edification of the credulous, the other the real, monarchical government.

With notable aid from corrupt Presbyterians, the House of Orange and its Amsterdam banking allies overthrew the British commonwealth in 1660, installing the Dutch puppets, the House of Stuart, upon the British throne. Those Stuarts proved to have several important defects as Dutch puppets. More narrowly, this being typical of the immorality and venality of the Scottish aristocracy generally, the Stuarts sold their favors wherever the market prices suited them, including circles around the French monarchy. More significantly, under James II the Stuart monarchy was reviving the efforts of the 1640-1660 period. The Dutch chose to reorganize the British government preemptively, under the direct supervision of the House of Orange.

The late seventeenth century House of Orange had no moral resemblance to its predecessor, William the Silent. The Dutch Neoplatonic humanism of William the Silent had been continued by the De Witt who was the ally of Benedict Spinoza. The wars between France and Holland had enabled the corrupted House of Orange to oust De Witt's humanists.

The late seventeenth century House of Orange, allied by marriage to the ruling, Black Guelph House of Hanover and otherwise thoroughly committed to Black Guelph policies in its own right, undertook to neutralize the republican ferment within the larger portion of the English population by instituting the form of theater known variously as British "constitutional monarchy" and British "liberalism." By giving the credulous British plebeians the thoroughly corrupted (to this day) British parliament with which to amuse themselves, the Black Guelph (Orange-Hanover) monarchy preserved to itself all it considered essential respecting the actual government of the United Kingdom.

By cultivated popular reputation, the British monarchy is a quaint enclave of ceremonial functions, plugging along quaintly on an annual household budget of a few millions. It, like its associates among the Black Guelph aristocratic families of continental Europe, is reputed by the credulous to exist principally to provide editorial copy for the society pages of certain news media, and for those quaint little women's magazines so popular among the most brutalized portions of the European population.

In reality, the British monarchy defines a domain of special powers and privilege outside the reach of existing practices of parliamentary control. It is screened from inquiry by the doctrine of *lese majeste* and by an arrangement known as the Official Secrets Act. Through the monarchy's own privileged financial activities, and through interface with and discretion of both the Bank of England and a select group of private merchant-banking

families, it is the centerpiece of one of the most powerful
financial institutions of the world.   It is otherwise armed
with extraparliamentary control of Britain's combined
official and unofficial intelligence services, and has de facto
as well as some nominal control over the British military.

This power is nominally located in the powers and
privilege of the incumbent monarch.   That aspect of the
matter has a certain importance, but represents far too
narrow a focus.   The British monarchy is best viewed as the
rallying point for an assemblage of oligarchical families,
both British and commonwealth nations, and also strata of
the allied oligarchical families of Europe.   These
oligarchical families, together with their most trusted
political servants, gather around and behind the screen of
the powers and privilege of the British monarchy.   Through
such and related means, and through the vast networks of
influence they have developed among many nations over
recent centuries, these combined forces control and deploy
one of the most powerful forces on earth, and the most
efficiently evil force existing today.

The neo-Aristotelian "secret knowledge" of these
oligarchical forces is transmitted to each generation within
the privileged strata in principally a threefold way.

First, the families themselves transmit their
oligarchical tradition, a certain way of viewing the world
and its matters of policy.   This transmission is both explicit
and implicit.   Some of the old families of Europe--on both
sides of the struggle--have organized memories going back
to Charlemagne's time.   More characteristically, the reach
of tradition is between approximately four and eight
centuries.   The explicit, formal aspect of the transmission

of family traditions centers around glossed genealogies, preferably illustrated with family portraits. More broadly, implicitly, the tradition is transmitted through a kind of "drill" governing the rearing of the young.

Second, the British oligarchical tradition and attitudes are shaped into forms of knowledgeable world outlook, in varying degrees of depth and breadth from case to case, by Oxford, Cambridge, and Sussex universities. (The London School of Economics is chiefly the center for recruiting foreigners to British intelligence service.) Together with these universities there are the public schools, which feed into the former. These institutions provide a center and model for the "gentlemen's education" of the oligarchies' young throughout the world.

Third, the articulation of policies and strategies agreeable to that tradition is accomplished through aid of various "think-tanks." Oxford, Cambridge, and Sussex universities include privileged domains which are the core of such arrangements. These are the institutions which coordinate the British Secret Intelligence Service (SIS or MI-6), MI-5, and the London Tavistock Institute. Other British institutions controlling British Policy, including its intelligence services' policies, include the Round Table, the Royal Institute of International Affairs (RIIA), and the International Institute for Strategic Studies (IISS).

The British intelligence services operate branches of IISS in many nations, including a part of the New York Council on Foreign Relations and the Aspen Institute in the United States. The Trilateral Commission is predominantly an arm of British intelligence services. The London Tavistock Institute controls the United Nations

Organization's World Federation of Mental Health, is the "mother" and continuing influence of the RAND Corporation, runs the Fabian operation against the United States' United Mine Workers Union, and many other institutions, including international terrorist networks, in many nations.

It is notable that many persons in high positions in the United States and other nations are both nominally and efficiently British intelligence services' agents-of-influence. The U.S. Labor Party has publicly documented the case of Henry A. Kissinger. The cases of Vice-President Walter A. Mondale, Senator Edward Kennedy, Zbigniew Brzezinski, Werner Michael Blumenthal, James R. Schlesinger, and many others could be added. The "Watergate" against President Richard M. Nixon was a monstrous hoax, set up from both inside and outside the administration by Kissinger, General Alexander Haig, and other British agents-of-influence, run on the outside largely by the networks of the Institute for Policy Studies and corrupt, complicit elements of the press, themselves either British agents outright or British agents-of-influence.

The United States is only the most important of the nations massively subverted by British intelligence services in this way.

THE "SECRET KNOWLEDGE"

The core of the knowledge guiding the overall direction of work of British intelligence services is "secret knowledge" based ultimately in the classics. This control of "secret knowledge" is centered in the collectivity represented by an inner intelligentsia of the oligarchical elite, a collectivity centered within Oxford and Cambridge universities.

On condition that one knows the classics and also the practical import of the knowledge embodied in them-- which, admittedly, few do, the "secret knowledge" of British intelligence services stands out as clearly as the sought-for letter stands out to the witting personality in the Poe story. Most relevant to this point is evidence proving the distinction between what Oxford and Cambridge know and what they profess publicly to believe.

The point is illustrated by the case of Thales's associate Anaximenes. "Everyone knows" that Anaximenes specified "air" to be one of the primary constituents of all substance. Yet, the Greek term which Oxford and Cambridge, in particular, have certified to signify "air" has approximately the same meaning as the modern German *Geist*, "mind" or "spirit," more precisely defined by context of usage. The fraud is so blatant that the translator who perpetrates it shows that he is engaged in a witting hoax.

Yet, the credulous Ph.D.'s and others who piously recite the fraud, and interpret Anaximenes from this standpoint, have not yet had their degrees revoked--least of all, not by Oxford and Cambridge.

Most of the widely accredited textbooks on classical philosophical and related topics are riddled with, indeed based upon blatant hoaxes to the same effect. To get at the real issues of the fourth century BC and earlier, and to trace the consequences of those continuing issues over subsequent centuries into the recent eighteenth century, one is obliged to discard the largest portion of the accredited "secondary sources" as either witting frauds or as a learned fool's glosses on the frauds he pathetically repeats.

Focusing for the moment only on the explicitly British conduct of such frauds, instances such as those we cited in connection with Anaximenes prove conclusively that the inner circles centered around Oxford and Cambridge are engaged in an effort to conceal the most vital issues of historical scholarship to their own advantage. By these means, they convert the most vital categories of historical knowledge into the "secret knowledge" of the inner elites, the elites not duped by the mythologies of the popular universities' classics and political science departments.

Once one knows that this fraud exists, sufficient primary and other suitable source-documentation exists to reconstruct the core of the truth in these matters--even acknowledging the masses of ancient documents which may be buried away from the honest scholar's view in one fashion or another. Consequently, the bare facts of the "secret knowledge" do indeed represent a likeness to the case of *The Purloined Letter*. The knowledge, admittedly widely scattered, exists in large measure, on condition one knows what one is seeking and in what sort of place it is located in which fashion.

That is the principal "secret" of the British intelligence services, the core of the body of "secret knowledge" through which the British and their accomplices have largely ruled the world during recent centuries.

We are not to be accused of singling out arbitrarily the seventh-through-fourth centuries BC in this connection. Once one has understood the crucial issues of that period of civilization, and knows how those issues shaped the course of all subsequent history, there exist with certainty no more important secrets to be discovered respecting past or present. That fact will be made clear in the course of this report.

We now cite one related, important case here. We cite the case of that influential hoax known as the Jewish religion.[3]

The modern Jewish religion originated not with the Kingdom of Solomon or earlier, but centuries later, as a synthetic cult created by the order of the Babylonians *and other non-Jews*. The first step in the fashioning of the Jewish religion was based on piecing together scraps of Mesopotamian legends (and anti-Phoenician and anti-Egyptian propaganda), with odd pieces of actual Babylonian and other history added to the mixture. The latter infusion gave a credible calendar to the otherwise fraudulent concoction. This original Mesopotamian hoax was reworked repeatedly, *always under the supervision of non-Jews*, with the basic structure of the Old Testament hoax completed during the Persian Empire period.

This hoax was first introduced into European languages about 230 BC, on the recommendation of the same Aristotelian Peripatetics who contrived the exotic cults of Ptolemaic Egypt, and on orders from the Ptolemies. That edition, of the "Seventy," is otherwise notable for the fact that it was produced in a variety of demotic Greek peculiar to such locations as the waterfront brothels of Egypt.[4]

Later, when Philo of Alexandria attempted to develop a Platonic version of Judaism (the roots of the later Sephardic tradition of Maimonides and Avencibrol), Philo avoided, for obvious political reasons, simply throwing out the mess before him. He attempted to circumvent the problem by the rabbinical, Pharasaical ruse of the "commentary," tolerating the text while fundamentally altering the reading to be attributed to it.

The Christian Apostles, confronted with the same general problem, rid Christianity of the worst implications of the Old Testament by emphasizing the "Dispensation of Christ," and warning against the dangers of the "concision." Christ had freed man from such barbarisms as the Old Testament. Only those sections of the Old Testament which pointed toward the coming of the Messiah or otherwise happened to coincide with Christianity were to be treated seriously.

It does not follow from this that the Apostles were in any fashion hoaxsters of the Aristotelian varieties. Apostolic Christianity always, and rightly so, regarded Aristotelianism as an organized force for evil, as did the greatest religious thinkers of the European Renaissance. Even Thomas Aquinas belatedly associated himself among such thinkers by acknowledging, during the period before his death, that all his preceding writings had been fundamentally in error. Apostolic Christianity and its leading continuations were always Platonic or Neoplatonic in respect of philosophical method. Aristotelian syncretic methods and Aristotelianism were introduced to

Christianity initially by way of the vestiges of the cult of Apollo, in the effort of the collapsing Roman Empire to develop an episcopal form of Christianity in conformity with pagan (Aristotelian) policies for design and use of state religious cults.

Although that view is not usually supported with such frankness by published church histories, many leading theologians, notably including Cardinal Nicholas of Cusa, are explicit on the problem of Aristotelianism. However, those theologians who concur with our judgment have generally regarded it as imprudent to disturb the naive faith of the ignorant with historical problems of this sort. This policy within Church circles intersects the fact that both the Platonics and Aristotelians adhered, for opposite reasons, to the doctrine of controlling the masses of people through mythologies. Since the point has also fundamental importance for the whole matter of this report, the Platonic view of the cited Church practice should be summarized at this point.

The Platonic method rightly distinguishes three qualities of knowledge, mental levels, among people.

The first, lowest condition of the human mind is the level of *simple belief*, belief premised on popular mythologies and prejudices, and on the state of ignorance concerning individual experience otherwise known as "common sense."

The second, next-higher level of knowledge is equivalent to the condition of *understanding* defined by Immanuel Kant, *the mere understanding*. Persons at this level have consistent knowledge of the ostensibly lawful features of practice in certain, various categories of human practice in general. This is a condition corresponding to the lowest level of what may be termed scientific knowledge. Such persons do not know why such categories exist, or how or why the ostensibly lawful principles appropriate to such categories are determined. They have merely practical knowledge of consistent cause-and-effect features of practice in those categories of experience in which they have been educated.

The third, highest level of human knowledge is *reason*, otherwise termed Plato's Socratic reason. It is only on this level that truth can be efficiently comprehended.

The knowledge of the two lower levels is necessarily mythological, false, or, as Spinoza specifies, "fictitious."

For such reasons, the Platonics judged mythologies twofoldly. All mythologies they knew to be inherently false (fictitious), *but no person could rise above mythologies except by attaining reason.* Therefore, in dealing with masses living at the inferior levels of mental life, it was deemed necessary to deal with them on the terms of mythological beliefs. The issue of practical politics therefore took the task oriented form of distinguishing among destructive and useful mythologies. Those forms of simple beliefs or mere understanding which tended to allow society to move in directions otherwise required by reason were deemed the tolerable class of mythologies. Those other mythologies, which tended toward evil consequences, were evil beliefs, which must be fought accordingly.

It is impossible to understand the central doctrinal issues among leading Christian theologians, from the apostolic period to present times, without taking that Platonic view inclusively into account. These theologians have been concerned *for themselves* and for determination of policy with the issues of truth according to reason. They have been, at the same time, otherwise concerned with popular mythologies, respecting chiefly the issue whether this or that popular belief led away from or toward the realization of the dictates of reason. Although the objective has been to bring all mankind into the state of reason (*atonement*), for immediate purposes the rule has been that this effort must be situated within terms of the problem defined by the simple beliefs of the ignorant.

The Aristotelians and their heirs, notably including Bernard of Clairvaux, Martin Luther and the Presbyterian leaders, had and continue an opposite policy concerning mythologies. The original Aristotelians were the intelligence-services arm of the oligarchies jointly controlling the court of Philip of Macedon and the contemporary Persian court of that time. Their objectives were to stop technological and scientific progress, and to create zero-growth synthetic mythologies as the simple beliefs of the ignorant masses. These efforts they regarded as the means to establish permanent world-rule by a

The Three Levels Of Human Consciousness

Simple Belief (above) *is the level of individual judgment defectively based on narrow experience and informed chiefly by prejudices and mythologies, corresponding to the "man of woman born" of Christian doctrine, and the image of "donkeyness" common in the Renaissance. It was illustrated by Renaissance humanist artist Albrecht Durer in his "Offer of Love," 1495.*

Understanding *(top of next page) is the level of judgment which comprehends fixed categories of scientific knowledge, corresponding to Christianity's enlightened state of knowledge effected by the Holy Spirit (Logos). Illustrated by a Durer woodcut showing two artists studying perspective, from his 1525 "Treatise on Measurement."*

Socratic Reason *(above) is knowledge based on the self-conscious comprehension of the process which characterizes the historical progress of scientific knowledge, a process identified in Christian theology with atonement in outlook with the Godhead, the creator. The humanist Durer depicted this level of mentation in his 1514 print, "St. Jerome in His Study."*

landlord-based oligarchy, deemphasizing cities in favor of the countryside, and maintaining "Malthusian" zero-growth, antitechnology policies against scientific progress. They have not altered that method or purpose to the present day.

The innermost belief of the leading Christian theologians with access to reason is typified by the outlook of the famous Abelard of the eleventh century AD. Where strict Aristotelians argued that God made himself impotent by creating inalterable laws for the universe--and hence only omniscient--Abelard defined the function of man's existence according to reason to be the helper of God in the continuing work of creation. Abelard located lawfulness in the lawfulness governing the ordering of continued creation. The exact opposite position was classically argued by the twelfth-century Bernard of Clairvaux, a point of importance we shall cover in the course of this report.

THE OUTER LIMITS OF "MARXISM"

Although Karl Marx made some genuine and important additions to human knowledge in general, Marx never succeeded in becoming part of the knowledgeable "inner elite." His doctrine has a collateral but no fundamental place within the "secret knowledge" of the elites.

Marx wrote that *all history is the history of class struggles.* To the extent this is partially true as a matter of description, it is otherwise so misleading as to be false as a guide for practice. Marx also wrote that the principal achievement of the emergence of industrial, urban-centered capitalist development was *to end the rule of society by "the idiocy of rural life."* The latter observation touches upon the "secret knowledge" of the elite, whereas the maxim cited before does not. Marx also bent, unfortunately, toward the view that the essential positive struggle of the human intellect *was toward "materialism," by way of but away from "idealism."* That latter view of Marx's is not only nonsensical, but prevented Marx from turning into the directions in which he might have discovered the "secret knowledge" he sought.

The true, primary determinants of the course of human history are expressed in the most concentrated form in the factional issue between the factions of Plato and Aristotle during the fourth century BC. All preceding and subsequent history is properly understood from that standpoint of conceptual reference, as we have already indicated and as we shall show in this report.

The partial truth buried under Marx's misunderstanding of the class struggle, a partial truth to which Marx himself was happily close for his practice, is that *the progress of humanity has been accomplished through the instrumentality of those social forces which, as social classes, have been oriented toward urban-centered technological, scientific and related cultural progress.* So far, Marx, like Lenin's Chernyshevskii, was correct.

However, that is an incomplete picture. As Plato emphasized, *the moving of the potentially positive social forces, e.g., positive social classes, has always depended upon the initiating role of a Platonic or Neoplatonic intelligentsia,* an intelligentsia which in every age has been activated by the seminal influence of a great, universal thinker. In today's preceding European history, Gottfried Wilhelm Leibniz was the last such universal intellect.

It is notable that Lenin's successful practice was governed by an approximation of the indicated principles.

Marx, unlike Leibniz, proceeded in ignorance of the "secret knowledge" of the Neoplatonic elite, and so Marx developed his important contributions to knowledge in a flawed, one-sided way. '

At points, Marx did come close to the "secret knowledge." Notably in his "Theses on Feuerbach" and in the first section, "Feuerbach," of *The German Ideology*, he touched upon the kernel of Neoplatonic knowledge. Had he not clung obstinately to certain important elements of Black Guelph mythology, his further development would have followed a much superior course. Pointing to those blunders of obsessive misbelief exposes the essential problem of Marx.

Marx's simplistic misconception of the class struggle in history and his pathetic view of "materialism" versus-"idealism" are essentially derivative of his acceptance of the myth certified as "history" through the broad influence of the Black Guelph, London-centered faction. In the wake of the 1815 Treaty of Vienna, the fraudulent account of history was made rapidly authoritative throughout Germany and other parts of Europe. Those were the accredited, prevailing "scholarly" views of Marx's time. Factually, they were more absurd than they were accredited. Marx's credulous acceptance of the main features of that hoax known as the "Ninth of Thermidor," and his related, crippling historiographical folly in tracing the progress of European intellectual life from Francis Bacon, are exemplary of the key to Marx's failures. For those and related reasons, the useful core of his work on methodology and political economy was situated within a containing belief in a prevailing, Black Guelph historiographical mythology.

Marx's foolish criticisms of the leading American economist, Henry C. Carey, efficiently illustrate the point.

Following the 1815 Treaty of Vienna, the American branch of the Neoplatonic movement of the eighteenth century was significantly contained and subverted increasingly overall, but it did not die out as a force as quickly as the Neoplatonic forces were crushed into obscurity in Europe itself. Through circles of "American Whigs" associated with John Quincy Adams, Henry C. Carey, and Henry Clay, a residue of the knowledge of the Neoplatonic heritage persisted, centering around knowledge of the fact that Britain continued to be the deadly enemy of both the United States and humanity in general, combined with the understanding that the British economy, despite its included industrial-capitalist feature, was governed by an anticapitalist oligarchy whose rule characterized the British economy as a whole.

Marx, as is generally known, viewed the British model as the classical empirical case of reference for the best approximation of industrial-capitalist development. That view was nonsensical, as Carey proved in his own writings. Marx, however, stubbornly rejected those abundant facts which refuted his credulous obsession on this point.

Marx's obsessive absurdities concerning history coincided with the flaws crippling his theory of knowledge. He, and Frederick Engels to greater extent, laid the basis in content for the foolish Soviet doctrines of perception and knowledge. The foolish doctrine that perceptions are the mirror-image of objects, and ideas predominantly the mirror-image of the objective state of development of the social-productive forces. This blunder is connected to Marx's ignorant overestimation of Francis Bacon and the eighteenth century "French materialists," as well as his incorporation of a total misrepresentation of European history up through the Treaty of Vienna.

OUR SPECIAL COMPETENCE

The time for tolerating the rule by fallacious doctrines of historiography has ended. The survival of the species demands a revival of the "secret knowledge" of the Neoplatonic elite. That knowledge must not only be revived, but as we do here, must be situated within and updated by appropriate terms of modern scientific knowledge.

The writer and his associates have come to this present state of knowledge fortunately, but not by accident. This writer, powerfully influenced at the outset of his teens by Leibniz's writings, has pursued that impulse by various pathways of activity, experience, and study all of his adult life. On the basis of his own initial, distinguishing accomplishments in political economy and method, beginning in the early 1950s, he subsequently, beginning in 1966, initiated a new kind of political organization *ex novo*, an organization based on those conceptions and their strategic-programmatic relevance for the developing world crisis.

Since early 1968 that organization has been in escalating direct conflict with British intelligence networks. In the course of that escalation matters have come to the present point, a point at which we have become, much as was Leibniz himself, one of the primary adversary-targets of the London-centered enemy forces. During the course of this escalating conflict, we developed what became a novel, specialized political intelligence capability. Partly because of and partly with aid of the capability, we have intersected increasing leading political forces, including other intelligence circles, in many parts of the world. Through this total experience, with aid of resources immediately and otherwise available for aid of our work, we have been able to produce the best conceptual overview of the British intelligence problem presently available.

Through the combined effects of our work in advanced aspects of the physical sciences and a decade's coordinated application of political-intelligence methods to crucial issues of history, we have in due course discovered ourselves to be much less a novel institution than we might otherwise have assumed to be the case. We have discovered that into the 1790s, the leading forces of the United States and the leading humanist forces of Europe were linked by common participation in international Neoplatonic networks, networks reaching back, essentially unbroken in continuity, over approximately three thousand years. Through such and related efforts, we have been able to revive, in suitably modem terms, the essential parts of the "secret knowledge" of that Neoplatonic elite.

Others among today's humanist elite already command important sections of that knowledge. In specific aspects of the matter, their knowledge is more richly developed than our own. Our distinction among these forces is that we have a grip on this knowledge in its universality. Our included task is to give that universal overview to all sections of that elite, and to obtain from them, in turn, the richer knowledge of particulars at their command.

Our combined forces, using this knowledge so revived among us, must rapidly inform other layers of the humanist elite--political figures, scientists, trade-union leaders, industrialists, outstanding farmers, and so forth--to the effect of creating the intellectually armed leadership force needed to defeat the horrors the London-centered Black Guelph faction now seeks to impose upon the world. We must mobilize ourselves to lead the human species once and forever out of the paranoid night of rule by mythologies.

Notes

1. Cf. Christopher White on the significance of the families, "The Noble Family," *Campaigner Special Report No. 11*, New York, 1978.

2. The majority of the following concerning Greek history is based upon or corroborated by the work of a task force coordinated by Criton Zoakos, plus work coordinated on behalf of the Wiesbaden Academy by George Gregory III.

3. Cf. Paul Arnest, "From Babylon to Jerusalem: The Genesis of the Old Testament," *Campaigner,* Vol. X, No. 4. Fall 1977, pp. 31-64.

4. Criton Zoakos.

I. THE LEGACY OF ARISTOTLE

The single most important "secret" of the Aristotelian, or neo-Aristotelian faction of the world's elite today is hidden behind the mythical image of Aristotle as an original philosophical thinker. In this chapter we shall trace this matter from Aristotle's time, emphasizing the role of his influence in the development of the Black Guelph faction, from the emergence of that faction around the leadership of the Pierleoni during the eleventh century AD, into the neo-Aristotelian developments associated chiefly with Francis Bacon and the late seventeenth century successors of Bacon around the British Royal Society. Once the contents of this present chapter and the next, on historiography, have been presented, the reader will have access to the most crucial of the "secrets" employed by humanity's enemies today.

The monstrously false report that Aristotle was the successor of Socrates and Plato, and also an important original thinker in behalf of scientific knowledge, is entirely a hoax without foundation in fact. Politically, philosophically, Aristotle was in all respects the enemy of Socrates and Plato, and also personally a chief enemy of Plato. The chief feature of Aristotle's character, the feature which is determining for everything else to be considered in that connection, is that like his contemporaries, the traitors Isocrates and Demosthenes, Aristotle was an agent working for the joint forces of the Persian and Macedonian courts.[1]

Although Aristotle was an agent of Philip of Macedon, he was--not inconsistently--a bitter enemy of Alexander the Great. Granted, Alexander and Aristotle maintained an interesting correspondence, and Philip did in fact appoint Aristotle Alexander's tutor. The textbooks which emphasize such selected bare facts for the deception of the credulous omit the additional facts; not only was Alexander Aristotle's philosophical and political adversary, but it was Aristotle's nephew who was convicted of attempting to murder Alexander by poisoning, and Aristotle's agents who did, according to authoritative sources of that time, finally assassinate Alexander.

The immediate background to the case of Aristotle is summarily as follows.

Philip of Macedon was a protege and ally of the leading general and others of the Persian imperial court.[2] The bankers of Mesopotamia, who centuries earlier had brought in the Persians to replace the Babylonians, had developed the view, by the mid-fourth century BC, that a new arrangement was needed. Their scheme centered about a policy of splitting the existing empire into two parts, both parts of which they would control. The western part of Anatolia, and the world otherwise west of the Euphrates, was to. become part of a new empire of the West. Philip of Macedon was their initial selection for creating the empire to grow to the west of the Euphrates.

First, they decided, Philip must subjugate Greece. To this purpose, Persian intelligence networks were deployed in behalf of Philip's conquest of Greece, and Persian advisors supplied to aid the process. Isocrates,

Demosthenes, and Aristotle were representative of such joint Persian-Macedonian spy-networks assigned to Athens.

This plot intersected the division over policy which had shaped the history of the Aegean since at least the eighth and seventh centuries BC. That division is reflected in a comparison of the irreconcilable outlooks of bucolic Hesiod and humanist Homer. Preceding the Persian conquests, the Ionian city-states had been leading representatives of the policy known as the "city-builders" policy, the current to which the doctrine of the modern Freemasons traces their origins. Under the leadership of "philosopher kings," such as the exemplary Thales, Ionian culture was dedicated by constitutions and intent to the promotion of urban-centered scientific and technological progress, and to the development of modes of production and of world trade to promote this cause, through colonies and other means, to promote this cause throughout the world. The opposite faction, centered traditionally in the priests and monetarist financier factions of Mesopotamia, opposed scientific progress, opposed urban centered cultural progress. They proposed a "zero growth," antitechnology policy, and the rule of society universally by a rural-centered, landlordism-based aristocracy, an oligarchy allied to monetarist financier circles.

This division was already an old one by the eighth into seventh century BC. As early as the middle of the third millennium BC, powerful city-states committed to urban centered technological progress and world-trade promotion existed. Prior to the fall of the Phoenician center of Tyre at the hands of the Persians' Mesopotamian predecessors, Phoenician culture had been over centuries a notable Eastern Mediterranean base for city-builders' policies and culture. After the conquest of Tyre, the Phoenicians' resources had been turned largely into instruments of Babylonian "zero-growth" policies. During this period, the political center of humanism in the Eastern Mediterranean region had shifted to Ionia and adjoining Lydia.

With the Persian subjugation of Lydia and Ionia, the center of humanist command among Greek-speaking peoples shifted to Athens. However, Athens was never homogenously a humanist city. The pro-rural-aristocracy or "zero-growth" faction of mainland Greece was also represented, and was to one degree or another allied with the Persians against the Ionian faction among the Greeks. The control center for the Persian faction in the Aegean region was the cult of Apollo, nominally centered in the banking nexus at Delphi.

Pericles is exemplary of Persian agents-of-influence in Athens. He may not have favored the Persian conquest of mainland Greece, but he did make every effort to ensure Persian subjugation of the Ionian cities, and launched the "WPA project" associated with his improvements of the Acropolis, as an antihumanist economic policy. Alcibiades is another case of a Persian agent-of-influence.[3] The zero-growth doctrine of Isocrates, the efforts of Macedonian paid-agent Demosthenes to aid Philip of Macedon in securing the desired war with Athens, and the spying and other black operations of Aristotle carried the tradition of the anti-humanist faction in Athens to its lawful extremes in degradation.

The cult of Apollo at Delphi is crucial. During the course of Persian campaigns against the Greeks and Lydians, the cult of Apollo is known, conclusively, to have run at least seven major operations in behalf of the Persians, including delaying the departure of Spartan forces to Marathon.[4]

The cult of Apollo should not be viewed as merely a curious institution of that period. It was on the one side the key monetarist financial institution of that period. On the other side it deployed two cults as covers for its intelligence operations as such. One of these cults was the cult of Apollo itself. The other principal cult was a subcult known as the Phrygian cult of Dionysus (in its Roman form, the cult of Bacchus). British intelligence services (as a whole) at the present date represent essentially a continuation of that cult and its characteristic methods and techniques. Aristotle and his Peripatetics were agents of that cult into Roman times, both as official Ptolemaic debt-collectors of the cult's financial operations, and as the controllers of the cult and its Dionysian offshoots.[5] Not only is British intelligence today collectively a continuation of that cult, but it is the mastery and replication of the methods and techniques of that cult which represent the innermost secrets of British intelligence services.

Before returning to the case of Alexander, we glance forward from the time of Alexander's death toward modern times, to afford the reader some sense of the importance of the cult of Apollo in ancient through modern history.

The cult of Apollo was not only an established institution in the Roman republic, but that institution managed the history of Rome down to the miserable end of

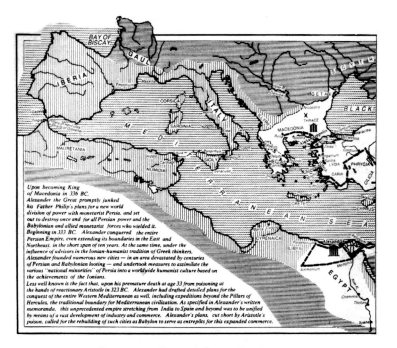

Upon becoming King of Macedonia in 336 BC, Alexander the Great promptly junked his Father Philip's plans for a new world division of power with monetarist Persia, and set out to destroy once and for all Persian power and the Babylonian and allied monetarist forces who wielded it. Beginning in 333 BC, Alexander conquered the entire Persian Empire, even extending its boundaries in the East and Northeast, in the short span of ten years. At the same time, under the influence of advisors in the Ionian-humanist tradition of Greek thinkers, Alexander founded numerous new cities — in an area devastated by centuries of Persian and Babylonian looting — and undertook measures to assimilate the various "national minorities" of Persia into a worldwide humanist culture based on the achievements of the Ionians.

Less well known is the fact that, upon his premature death at age 33 from poisoning at the hands of reactionary Aristotle in 323 BC, Alexander had drafted detailed plans for the conquest of the entire Western Mediterranean as well, including expeditions beyond the Pillars of Hercules, the traditional boundary for Mediterranean civilization. As specified in Alexander's written memoranda, this unprecedented empire stretching from India to Spain and beyond was to be unified by means of a vast development of industry and commerce. Alexander's plans, cut short by Aristotle's poison, called for the rebuilding of such cities as Babylon to serve as entrepôts for this expanded commerce.

Alexander The Great's "Grand Design"

Map Text: *Upon becoming King of Macedonia in 336 BC, Alexander the Great promptly junked his father Philip's plans for a new world division of power with monetarist Persia, and set out to destroy once and for all Persian power and the Babylonian and allied monetarist forces who wielded it. Beginning in 333 BC, Alexander conquered the entire Persian Empire, even extending its boundaries in the East and Northeast, in the short span of ten years. At the same time, under the influence of advisors in the Ionian-humanist tradition of Greek thinkers, Alexander founded numerous new cities--in an area devastated by centuries of Persian and Babylonian looting--and undertook measures to assimilate the various "national minorities" of Persia into a*

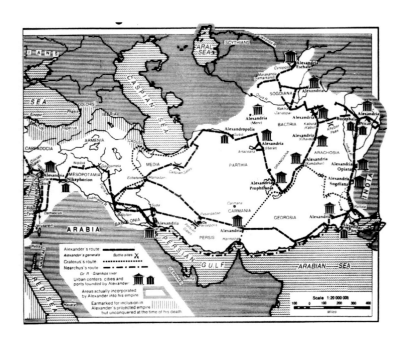

worldwide humanist culture based on the achievements of the Ionians.

Less well known is the fact that, upon his premature death at age 33 from poisoning at the hands of reactionary Aristotle in 323 BC, Alexander had drafted detailed plans for the conquest of the entire Western Mediterranean as well, including expeditions beyond the Pillars of Hercules, the traditional boundary for Mediterranean civilization. As specified in Alexander's written memoranda, this unprecedented empire stretching from India to Spain and beyond was to be unified by means of a vast development of industry and commerce. Alexander's plans, cut short by Aristotle's poison, called for the rebuilding of such cities as Babylon to serve as entrepôts for this expanded commerce.

City-Builders Of Antiquity

The basis for the urban revival in both Medieval Europe and the Islamic world was laid by the faction of Mediterranean city-builders which can be traced continuously back to the economic and cultural revival in Phoenicia beginning around 1000 BC, the start of the Iron Age. The Phoenicians set out to colonize the western Mediterranean, and Phoenician civilization rapidly reproduced itself among the Greeks of Ionia, and continued by Plato's Academy. After the death of the humanist Alexander, the impulse of the city-builders' policies was kept alive by humanist networks operating within fascist Rome. They emerged amid the collapse of Rome in the form of Neoplatonism and apostolic Christianity, to lay the basis for the revival of civilization in the political-religious organizations which produced the Islamic Renaissance and the Holy Roman Empire.

Phoenicia

King Hiram of Tyre (c. 1025-950 BC)

King Solomon of Israel (c. 1000-925 BC)

King Ahab of Israel (d. 853 BC)

Ionia

Homer (c. 750/725 BC)

Psammetichus I, Pharaoh of Egypt (reigned 663-609 BC)

Thales of Miletus (c. 840-546 BC)

Solon of Athens (c. 638-559 BC)

Anaximander of Miletus (c. 611-547 BC)

Heraclitus of Ephesus (c. 544-484 BC)

Parmenides of Elsa (c. 540-470 BC)

Aeschylus (529-456 BC)

Democritus of Abdera (c. 460-370 BC)

Platonic Academy

Socrates (470-399 BC)

Plato (427-347 BC)

Archytas of Tarentum (fl. c. 375 BC)

Alexander the Great (356-323 BC)

Euclid (fl. c. 300 BC)

Archimedes of Syracuse (287-212 BC)

Antigonus Gonatas, King of Macedonia (reigned 283-239 BC)

Alexandria

Philo of Alexandria (c. 25 BC-50 AD)

Paul of Tarsus (1st century AD)

Plotinus (203-269 AD)

Origen (185-254 AD)

The Lighthouse at Alexandria, from an ancient coin

Latin Fathers

St. Ambrose of Milan (340-397)

St. Augustine of Hippo (354-430)

the Empire.[6]   It was for this reason that Rome's only contribution to human culture was the military system which Rome perfected in the aftermath of the Punic wars. Roman law was, and is, a hideous, antihumanist concoction explicitly following the specifications of the cult of Apollo as explicated by Aristotle et al. The Roman aristocracy was promoted by the cult of Apollo as an expression of the "Persian model" doctrine of the court of Philip of Macedon. The fall of the Roman republic was the result of the cult of Apollo's placing its chips on the Marian faction (Caesar), and developing a Dionysian cult among the Roman plebeians in Rome, to provide Caesar with the same organization of a social base of power as the later Mussolini and Hitler.

After the assassination of Alexander by Aristotle's agents, a humanist republic was established in Athens by a general who was otherwise one of Alexander's closest supporters. The Peripatetics were kicked out of Athens at that point, and moved their center of operations, lock, stock and library, to the Egypt of Alexander's enemy, Ptolemy. There, they created the exotic synthetic cults of Egypt (e.g. the Isis-Osiris cult), translated the Old Testament into waterfront brothel Greek, and enjoyed management fees as debt-collectors of the cult of Apollo's financial operations. Acting through their branch at Rome, the Ptolemian head office of the Peripatetic cult secured the movement of the Roman legions into mainland Greece, to destroy the last vestiges of Ionian political rule there. The visits of Julius Caesar and Marc Antony to Cleopatra's Egypt fall under the same category of significance.

During the last decade of the eighteenth century, British intelligence services deployed agents Danton and Marat into Paris, organizing a rabble from among lumpenized peasant-vagabonds drawn into Paris as elements of a Dionysian cult, *down to the detail of Phrygian caps.*[7] British intelligence's creation of fascism in Italy and Weimar Germany, the more recent development

The Paris mob, organized by British intelligence on the paradigm of the Phrygian-Dionysiac mobs of antiquity, was celebrated by the "neo-classical" painters who emerged from the French Revolution. In Eugene Delacroix's "Liberty at the Barricades" (1830), "Liberty" is depicted approvingly as a Dionysian maenad, and she and her fellow rioters are portrayed with the detail of the Phrygian caps which the British furnished their lumpenized Parisian stooges.

of the rock-drug counterculture, the Maoist organizations, international terrorism and the "zero growth environmentalism" are a replication of the same method and techniques used by the ancient cult of Apollo in managing its Phrygian cult of Dionysus in the Aegean littoral.

The promotion of Roman law in eighteenth-century France was centered around British-intelligence protege Montesquieu, just as Voltaire, another British agent, in his historical frauds, slanders against Leibniz. etc., reflected British imitation of the techniques used to the same purpose against humanism by the cult of Apollo during the fifth and fourth centuries BC.

The technology of culture has not changed profoundly since the fourth century BC. The essential methods and techniques of the cult of Apollo, and its continuation at Oxford and Cambridge have not altered in a single essential feature. The objectives. the policies. the methods remain essentially the same.

During the middle fourth century BC the influence of the Ionian faction in Athens centered around the work of Socrates and Plato. The Academy of Athens was no mere teaching institution. Nor was Plato's decade of occupation with the republic-project for Syracuse exceptional in principle (the *Republic*). The participants in the Academy at Athens were drawn from all areas of Greek influence in the Mediterranean. The regular work of the Academy included the development of constitutional forms government for the nations of that culture.[8]

One of Aristotle's chief assignments as a Macedonian-Persian spy in Athens was his participation in the destruction of the Academy. The earlier judicial murder of Socrates was no eccentric autochthonous affair of Athenian internal life. Aristotle's other duties there were principally those of a spy for Philip of Macedon's interest, a duty which he and other Peripatetic agents of the cult of Apollo performed in various places.

On the basis of Aristotle's demonstrated deep--one should say, abysmal--commitments and skills as an enemy of the human species, his patrons assigned him to various locations. In addition to his services as a spy and assassin, he played a leading role in the literary activities for which the Peripatetics are ordinarily reputed. However, contrary to what is believed by the credulous, and taught by both hoaxsters and fools, Aristotle was not engaged in the progress of knowledge. The literary activities of the Peripatetics were chiefly dedicated to a scheme for eliminating the influence of scientific method from civilization.

The technique employed to that malignant purpose was one which post-1670 Europe would justly term "encyclopedic." The doctrines of all existing branches of knowledge were *rewritten,* with the additional distinction of being recodified in such a fashion as to eliminate as far as possible all trace of the scientific method, and to mystify the origins of existing knowledge in this and related ways. Aristotle, like other members of the Peripatetics, was assigned to various locations. In each location he or others would take down a section of the existing body of knowledge from some relevant source authority, and would then proceed to recodify that information according to the doctrine of the cult of Apollo.

This was exactly the technique employed, initially under the coordinating supervision of John Locke, to develop the British Royal Society, and launch the Scottish

Encyclopedia Britannica. It is now documented that Isaac Newton made not a single original useful contribution to scientific knowledge. In fact, he was almost fully occupied with his efforts to master "black magic"--as the surviving archives show him to have been actually engaged at the time his associates later fraudulently alleged him to have developed his calculus.[9] Insofar as Newton (and Boyle) drew their materials from English sources, this involved not only appropriating as their own work of Wallis and Barrow, but shamelessly and repeatedly plagiarizing the work of Hooke. Newton's physics was, in the main obtained through Hooke's completing the mathematization of the discoveries already completed by William Gilbert, Kepler, and Galileo, and adding in the discovery (inertia) contributed by Gottfried Leibniz. Leibniz and Huygens were among the contemporaries most frequently plagiarized by the Royal Society during that period. Rightly could Newton inscribe his *Principia*, "hypothesis is not necessary"; what need has a plagiarist of hypothesis? However, the slogan, "hypothesis is not necessary" has another significance. Like Aristotle's Peripatetics, the purpose of the Royal Society's circulation of scientific works was to eliminate scientific progress, by outlawing the principle of rigorously formulated crucial hypothesis (ritually denounced as "metaphysics") in favor of that banalizing doctrine known as "the principle of the inductive sciences."

Such antiscientific literary undertakings aside, the principal empirical pursuit of the Peripatetics in matters of knowledge was the subject of botany. This is the one aspect of Aristotle's writings which stands out as having some explicit content of interest in the development of knowledge. Why the exception in this case? The interest in botany was essentially political, in a manner of speaking. The specialty of the Peripatetic assassins was poisoning.

ARISTOTELIAN RELIGIOUS CULTS

Apart from the work of spying, "encyclopedism," and poisoning, the principal production of the Peripatetics included the production of new religious and quasi-religious cults. (It is not entirely without significance that that portion of the Thames suffering the misfortune to lie near Oxford is named the "Isis.") We have already referred to the synthetic cults of Egypt (e.g.. the Isis-Osiris cult, and others) produced by the Peripatetics under the Ptolemies. The same methods used to this purpose by the Peripatetics have been continued by their emulators down to the present day. Such British intelligence-service creations as the Hare Krishna cult, the "Children of God," and the so-called "Moonies" are only the most obvious and notorious such concoctions. The Maoist organizations of North America and Western Europe are based on the same methods and techniques of cult design, as is the British intelligence-created rock-drug counterculture, the "environmentalist" movement, and the overlapping organization of international terrorism, represents only one form of such Babylonian synthetic religious cults. It is not the details of these cults, that ought to occupy our attention here, but rather the characteristic features of such cult-design from then to the present time.

The methods of creating synthetic religious cults as instruments of state domestic and foreign policies is known in some significant detail since Babylon. The original synthesis of what later becomes the Jewish religion

The usual form of the religious cult down to the Christian era was associated with a pantheon of polymorphs, gods and semi-deities whose images combined either features of several animals into one form, or which combined human and animal forms. The essential, political effect of such religious cults is to destroy the concept of a qualitative distinction between man and the lower beasts. These were, indeed, all "greenie" religious cults. The interesting distinction of the Jewish cult, among the usual, polymorphous productions of the Babylonian "foreign office," is evolution over subsequent developments away from the polymorphous image of worship. However,.otherwise, the Babylonian-created cult of Judaism was the most thorough of the ancient zero-growth cults.

Although the following involves an included element of speculation, the elements of knowledge drawn upon as circumstantial evidence are valid without question. Only the specific, historical connection we interpolate for further investigation of the matter is properly considered speculative.

It is known that the Israel and adjoining nations of the period of Saul, David, and Solomon--especially Solomon's Israel, were buffer-states of the Phoenicians (e.g.. Tyre). In a manner consistent with city-builders' policies, the backward people of Israel had been brought up, largely, to a civilized state through a city-builder program. (Hence, the Freemason legend of the early Freemasons as Phoenician-trained builders of the temple of

Dionysian cults, yesterday and today: throughout the centuries a basic item of antihumanist social control technique.

Solomon.) It is also known that there was no trace of "Judaism" as later defined, but rather a strong influence of the cult of Baal otherwise widespread throughout the region, together with Phoenician cults.

We also know, from the standpoint of epistemology, that the characteristic philosophical outlook of Thales, Heraclitus, et al. is an expression of the world-outlook upon which the city-builders' culture converges. Hence, philosophical beliefs converging upon the views of the Ionians, Socrates, and Plato were in fact influential among the leading strata of eastern Mediterranean city-builders prior to the Ionian period, including therefore leading strata in Israel.

The function of the Babylonian creation of the Jewish religious cult was to transform the people of Israel into an advance-post Babylonian, puppet-state for Babylon's war against Tyre. Consequently, the Babylonians were constrained by the kinds of religious belief which already existed in an area strongly influenced by Phoenician culture. Hence, the ordinary sort of polymorphous-image cults might not have succeeded in that region.

We know also that the city-builders and their antihumanist adversaries often did not attempt to directly uproot existing mythologies, but rather to recodify existing mythologies in such a way as to serve the policy of the state. The mythology was adjusted to embody, as a mythology, the impulses appropriate either to a city-builders' or antihumanist policy. The thrust, on the humanist, or city-builders' side, throughout the known sources, is toward the deified human hero or heroine, for which the Herakles-Prometheus model is typical: the giver of knowledge (reason) to a whole people. The antihumanist policy emphasizes the opposite policy: it proposes the irrationality of the deities, it insists upon the unfathomable mystery of the order of the universe. On this basis, we can not confidently assume that the existence of image-worship *in itself* meant one thing or the other. Only the features of image-worship or other forms of worship which are characteristically Platonic or anti-Platonic are solid evidence.

The durability of the synthetic religion of Judaism, through its various evolutions up to the Christian era and its survival after the onset of that era, reflects the cumulative, "environmental" selective effect of the Platonic-Neoplatonic revolts against the older form of religious polytheistic antihumanist cults. This revolt took its decisive form in the rise of Christianity, which was politically and philosophically a Platonic-Neoplatonic upsurge within the Hellenistic world against the monstrous evil represented by the Roman Empire and Roman law. This same principle is reflected in the original political thrust of the Prophet Muhammad, and in the emergence of the Ismaili current within Islam. During that latter period Judaism itself was divided between the reactionary "orthodox" currents and the tendency for humanistic, Neoplatonic transformation of Judaism. The emergence of the humanistic Sephardic current out of the Ismailite Judaic faction, and the emergence of Maimonides, Avencibrol, et al. of the Toledo school, reflect the course of the latter aspect of the development.

In general, the main course of development of religious and philosophical belief among humanist and humanist-influenced currents, has been away from the polytheistic, image-centered doctrines toward the *Logos*-principle, and toward the trinity doctrines as exemplified by the internal determinations of the Platonic dialogue. The survival of Judaism coincides with the effect of such circumstances. It is merely, in itself, a plastic *form* of belief, which can be made either humanistic or antihumanistic, and serves the latter purpose with. the advantage of being ancient, and also largely free of the incredible, hated polytheistic forms which were discarded in the wake of the Mediterranean worldwide hatred of Roman Latin imperial order.

Another decisive feature of Judaism is the ancient association of nominal Jews with banking. Throughout the period from Babylon into the persecution of the Jews during the thirteenth century and afterwards in Europe, one faction of Jews was continuously associated with monetarist policies of finance throughout the Mediterranean littorals, whereas the other faction, the medieval Sephardic faction, especially during the Christian era, was associated with Ismaili humanist policies of opposition to monetarist financial policies. Despite the inevitable, large-scale assimilation of Jews into the mainstream of the cultures in which they were situated, a kernel of Jewry remained defined and otherwise self-defined as "outsiders" to the mainstream of the cultures in which they resided. (And, so forth and so on. The relevant points should be clear.) This fact we shall encounter below, in connection with the Pierleoni.'

On their side of the matter of religion, the work of the Peripatetics was directed to the same objectives as their frauds in knowledge generally. In philosophy, the Peripatetics sought to poison the second level of Platonic knowledge, the mere understanding, against knowledge of the scientific method (reason). In religion, they treated the lowest state of human knowledge, simple beliefs of the ignorant masses, to the same purpose. The object was to promote irrationalist beliefs agreeable to state policies of zero-growth and monetarist-oligarchical rule.

The same sort of project was launched by British intelligence services during the 1920s, with the evil Bertrand Russell the central figure in this operation. During the 1920s, Russell, as a principal spokesman for the effort, laid out a spectrum of projects, all aimed to bring about a "new dark age," through which an oligarchy-ruled "feudalist" utopia could be established on a world scale.

Russell proposed the end of progress in basic scientific knowledge. British radical-empiricists and their Vienna positivist-energeticist collaborators ganged up against Max Planck, Erwin Schroedinger, de Broglie and others in aid of this project. This represented an attempted "final solution" to the attack against "continental science," which had been continuous British policy since the wretched Francis Bacon's attack on William Gilbert and the British Royal Society's vendettas against Descartes and Leibniz. A key figure in this was British agent Niels Bohr. Bohr's hideous conduct toward Schroedinger and others, the founding of the irrationalist "Copenhagen School," and the hooligan uproar against leading scientific thinkers at the 1920s Solvay conference, were leading features of the Russell-linked operations against scientific progress.

The continuous campaign of the British against nuclear and fusion-energy development, from the World War II period to the present day, is partly the Black Guelph oligarchy's campaign against technological progress, and also a continuation of Russell's project for destroying the progress of science from within.

Russell also proposed the application of existing scientific technology to the purposes of mass mind-control, including the development of drugs for mass use for this purpose. Aldous Huxley's *Brave New World* and others' leading roles in promoting psychedelic drugs and drug-cultures are part of the implementation of that British Black Guelph project for mass drug addiction.

Russell was more directly active, from that point onward, in the development of what became known as "linguistics." This is the form of "linguistics" most popularly associated with the name of former Rand Corporation associate, Professor Noam Chomsky. Russell, working closely with longstanding British intelligence operative Karl Korsch, and with Carnap and others, launched linguistics in the United States during the 1930s, also in intersection with the work of the fascist sociologist, social-work "brainwasher" Dr. Kurt Lewin. Noam Chomsky, whose work is used prominently, and directly, for the development of explicitly brainwashing techniques, is a direct protege of the apparatus set up under Russell's leadership.

Russell-Korsch-Carnap-Chomsky linguistics extend the methods of synthetic religious-cult building of the Peripatetics to an extreme. The cognitive feature of the use of language is systematically outlawed wherever linguistics methods are employed. The philosophical outlook of the cult of Dionysus is central to linguistics. There is no universal lawfulness, but only the heteronomic impulses and desires of the individual and small group. In other words, the doctrines of Thomas Hobbes, also perceptively adopted by the Nazi regime as appropriate to its character.

Maoism, the rock-drug counterculture, "environmentalism," and the "philosophical" environment of British-created international terrorism and its sympathizers, are all forms of the cult of Dionysris developed during recent decades with majority complicity from a corrupt press and universities in the promotion and application of Chomskyian linguistics.

MACEDONIAN POLICIES

The Aristotelians were essentially distinguished by their determination to wipe out the human race's memory of Ionian (i.e.. Platonic) scientific methods, and to eliminate the influence of humanist, city-builder policies. They, as agents of the joint Persian Macedonian policies of the cult of Apollo, were committed to what the Macedonian court of Philip identified as the "Persian model." This was, as we noted above, a policy of suppressing urban-centered culture and technological progress, in behalf of the rule of society by a landlord oligarchy allied to the monetarist bankers centered in Delphi and Mesopotamia. The Macedonian court thus expressed the same policies and sociological outlook as the British Black Guelph oligarchy of the past centuries to date.

Ironically, the sodomy prevailing in the court of Macedon contributed to Philip's undoing. A member of his court had been gang-sodomized at the order of another.[10] Philip not only refused to punish the perpetrator, but, instead, appointed the criminal to the governorship of a province. This motivated the victim to become the assassin of Philip at a most appropriate point in history, on the very eve of the intended implementation of the joint project of Philip and the Persian court circles.

In this connection, we should reemphasize, what we have outlined above in connection with Aristotelian religious cults.

The commonplace blunder of professed Marxists and others in assessing British policies is the mistaken assumption that the ruling forces of the British oligarchy are motivated by specifically capitalist impulses. It is of course the case that the British oligarchy and its global allies live in a world in which the industrial capitalist forms of manufacturing, agriculture, trade, and culture are the premise upon which human existence depends. It is also true that world rule to this date in recent modern history has been feasible only to the extent that representatives of the Black Guelph oligarchy controlled the financial power, and state material power adapted to industrial-capitalist development. However, to conclude from such and related evidence, evidence valid up to a point, that the British oligarchy's motives are subsumed under the rubric of "capitalist" is the grossest of blunders, of incompetencies.

The Guelph (Welfen) were originally a bucolic German aristocratic house, associated with the rule of Franconia, with branches in Italy. During the eleventh century, through an alliance among Roman banking families centered around the Pierleoni, including Matilda of Tuscany and the ruling house of Lotharingen (Lorraine), the oligarchical faction of the present millennium acquired the name Guelph through the marriage-connection of Matilda of Tuscany's House to the Welfen house. In the course of developments following the Guelph defeat of the Hohenstaufen House (Frederick Barbarossa through Frederick II) during the events of 1266-1268 AD, there arose the Guelph-Ghibelline (Ghibelline=Italianized Waibling, as Guelph was Italianized Welf) disputes. In the internal struggles within Italy (and elsewhere) at the onset of the fourteenth century, the Italian branches of the Guelph aristocracy split into a "White Guelph" and a "Black Guelph" faction, the former won to the humanist policies otherwise associated with the Ghibelline (Hohenstaufen-Waibling) faction. Dante Alighieri was a leading thinker for the former faction. From the early fourteenth century, the antihumanist oligarchical faction of Europe has represented the continuity of the Black Guelph faction of Dante's time.

The Capetian House in France, the later Hapsburgs (whose significance dates from the emergence of the Black Guelph faction of which that household is predominantly a part), and the majority of the aristocratic households of Europe have been predominantly a conscious continuation of the traditions and policies of the Guelph faction of the eleventh century and its Black Guelph continuation since the onset of the fourteenth century. The term "black nobility" in today's Italy refers with approximate exactness to the present-day continuation of the Black Guelph oligarchical families in Italy.

Aristocratic families do not necessarily mean Black Guelph, however. The case of the Bourbon-Borbon house of France and Spain illustrates the point.

The humanist tradition within the French monarchical houses dates from the fifteenth century Louis XI--whose father, Charles, was a despicable, Guelphish monster. The humanist (city-building) policies of Louis XI were continued by the House of Navarre during the sixteenth century, and continued by the seventeenth century *politiques*--Richelieu, Mazarin, and Colbert. In fulfillment of Richelieu's anti-Hapsburg policy, France of Mazarin et al., allied with Cromwell's English commonwealth, finally humbled the Hapsburgs in 1653, leading to the Borbon succession in Spain.

The Bourbon-Borbon monarchs were a mixed lot, as typified by the case of Louis XIV. The Bourbon tendency expressed by Louis XIV's minister Colbert--and by Descartes and Huygens--was one current. The rural aristocratic input into Louis XIV was the Guelphish side. The case of the ill-fated clock-hobbyist, Louis XVI, less interesting than his exceptional contemporary, Joseph II of Austria's Hapsburgs, illustrates the case of monarchs pulled toward the humanist side of policies, just as the Duke of Orleans was not only a raving Guelph, but an agent of the British monarchy.

Prior to the hegemony of Godoy in the Spanish court, the Spanish Borbon court of the mid-eighteenth century was a center of influence of the "French faction," to which the painter, Francisco Goya was attached. This faction of the Spanish Borbon court developed a humanist, city-building project-policy for "Greater Spain," and contributed in a vital way to the fostering of the humanist currents in such later Latin-American nations as Mexico.

The English Tudors are another example of the problem. The case of Richard III of England is open to fresh scrutiny. The case of Warwick is of more immediate interest. In any event, the accession of the Tudors involved the influences associated with Louis XI of France, and apart from peculiarities of some of the Tudor monarchs as such, the humanists gathered around the Dudley family are

The Spanish court under the reign of Charles III [1759-1788] (left) was a center of the "French faction" of European humanists associated with Benjamin Franklin which battled the English-led monetarists for hegemony in Europe in the late eighteenth century. A notable figure in that court was the humanist painter Francisco Goya, whose art was a part of that struggle. In 1780, the young Goya portrayed Charles III--the patron of humanists--in an informal and affectionate hunting pose. Following Charles's death, humanism in Spain waned as the star of Manuel de Godoy, (above) the lover of the new queen, rose, and Goya's art grew more sharply polemical. His 1801 portrait effectively captures the sadism and conceit of the fat-faced and licentious Godoy.

key to everything decent that occurred in England during the sixteenth century and immediately thereafter.

The accurate view of the role of the European aristocracy and monarchical families in general is twofold. First of all, these families were divided overall and internally on fundamental issues of policy. Some representatives were deeply committed to humanist or antihumanist policies. Others vacillated under pressure of opposite factions--as did Elizabeth I of England. Second, the point against the institution of monarchy made by Machiavelli and emphasized, in denouncing both monarchy and democracy, by Thomas Paine, that the hereditary monarchy, subject to radical changes in the policy-outlook of the state's chief, hereditary executive from generation to generation, proved itself to be intolerable to the humanist interest.

The case of Russia's czars is also exemplary. The humanist leaders of later Byzantium, the Paleologues, rose to power through a persisting conspiracy of the humanists of central Europe. Henry V of Germany, in approximately 1106 AD, assigned a humanist aristocratic family of Italy (from Viterbo, outside Rome) to infiltrate the establishment of Byzantium. As the Paleologues, this humanist aristocratic family gained the rulership of Byzantium during the thirteenth century, holding that power until a Turkish conquest (1453) arranged by the perfervidly Aristotelian patriarch of the eastern church and the bankers of Rome traditionally controlling the Papacy. However, among the positive heritages of the Paleologues was their humanist influence in Russia, establishing the policy of Ivan III, and of Ivan IV (The Awesome).[11] Despite the efforts of Ivan IV's political heir, Boris Godunov, the Hapsburg led evil then seizing continental Europe led to the undoing of much of the humanist efforts of the czars, producing a post-Boris period of chaos which ended only with the emergence of the Romanovs.

From Peter I, the Romanovs were under the influence, increasingly, of Anglo-Dutch penetrations of the Russian court. Barring the curious case of the death of Catharine in the eighteenth century, every Czar died a sudden death, exactly at the point Anglo-Dutch policy interest prescribed this demise.[12] English physicians attached to the Czarist household were not irrelevant to such abrupt departures from life of the Czars, nor was it irrelevant that British intelligence services, conduiting funds through their agent Alexander Herzen, funded Bakunin and controlled the Russian anarchist movement and its terrorist offshoot.

Nor is it astonishing that when Count Witte was embarked on a policy for promoting the industrial development of Russia in closer relationship to Germany, the Russian 1905 Revolution was organized with a leading role of Anglo-Dutch (Samuel) agent Alexander Helphand-Parvus, and with a leading role by Parvus's protege of that moment, Leon D. Trotsky. (Karl Radek, N. Bukharin, and G. Riazanov were agents of the Anglo-Dutch-Royal Dutch Shell-intelligence networks featuring Parvus. The "doctor's plot" against Stalin's life was probably no exaggeration at all.)

As Thomas Paine emphasized, monarchy is an unacceptable form of government in the humanist interest, but sections of the aristocracy and monarchs have been, nonetheless, dedicated humanists.

Exemplary of the latter point is the case of the Salian Holy Roman emperors, from Otto I through Henry IV, and the Hohenstaufen emperors, from Frederick Barbarossa through Frederick II. The thrust of these Holy Roman emperors was earlier expressed by Charlemagne. They were predominantly humanists, city builders. The policies otherwise expressed by Abelard were embedded in the building of urban-centered culture and trade-routes, north-south and east-west by the Salian emperors. The urban culture of Europe did not emerge by some spontaneous principle within "feudalism," but because leading "dirigist" monarchs and others steered the application of "national" financial and economic resources to bring this about, and because those same potentates and others fostered humanist education, including energetic programs for establishing great universities, and collecting the greatest minds available and the most valuable documents available for this purpose.

The ruling elites of civilization have very long memories, and represent objectives and policies which have not changed essentially over thousands of years.

For example of the follies to be brushed aside, consider Karl Marx's nonsensical, argument advanced in his effort to brush aside the evidence of the American Revolution. Marx argued that English capitalism was old and matured, whereas American capitalism was young, primitive and lacking the problem of high relative organic composition of industrial capital which prevailed in "more matured" England. Factually, Marx's observation was purely conjectural and false.[13]

During the eighteenth century, despite the continuation of Guelphish, "feudal" relations in the French countryside, French industrial development and French rates of industrial expansion and technological progress were in advance of those in an England which was relatively stagnating under Guelph policies of the Hannoverian monarchy. During the latter half of the eighteenth century, both wages and social productivities of labor in the English-speaking American colonies and the young United States were significantly higher than those in England, just as American literacy rates were then more than double those in England. Wherever industrial capital was introduced in the United States the issue which was central to the American Revolution--the quality of American technology was significantly superior to that in England. Marx's argument, that the organic composition of capital had overtaken the more matured England, was sheer nonsense.

The "high organic composition" of British capital was not a result of industrial accumulation, but of the British financial debt, incurred in the effort to prevent continental Europe and England itself from developing an industrial-development-centered policy.

As Alexander Hamilton's 1791 *Report on Manufactures* proves clearly enough, and as Henry C. Carey stated the point bluntly and accurately, the British System was not an industrial capitalist model, but a "mixed economy," in which the interest and dynamic of industrial capital was subordinated through the monarchy and oligarchy to parasitical landlord interest, an interest which took "primitive accumulation" from rural landholdings as its point of reference for policy. The British physiocratic doctrine, like its French imitators, expressed that point of view exactly.[14]

The same point is exposed most nakedly by the Ford Foundation's 1964 "Triple Revolution" report, advocating a "post-industrial society," and the coordinated launching of the international "environmentalist" ferment by British intelligence services' networks beginning the autumn of 1969. The targets of these British intelligence services' operations have been precisely industrial development, industrialist profits, and so forth. Excepting London's (and its monetarist allies') perfervid preoccupation with strengthening its control of the world's nominal financial wealth, London's policy is perfervidly anticapitalist.

What sort of an idiot is it that would attempt to turn up a *capitalist* motive for the policies of British intelligence services and the British government?

The ruling, Black Guelph oligarchy of Britain, together with those oligarchical families (aristocratic and quasi-aristocratic) to which it is allied outside Britain, is dedicated essentially, by its own statement on the matter, to bringing about a "new dark ages," out of which depopulated globe (reduced willfully to the order of as few as 1 billion persons through wars and economic genocide by the close of the present century), the permanent rule of the world by "feudal" oligarchical families is established. In short, the British monarchy and the forces rallied about it represent nothing but the effort to implement the "Persian model" policies of the court of Philip of Macedon in a modern technological context. That is the project Henry Kissinger, James R. Schlesinger, W. Michael Blumenthal, Zbigniew Brzezinski and other British agents-of-influence within the United States represent now as emphatically as the Churchills, Mountbattens, Russells, and such British social-democrats as Denis Healey and Roy Jenkins.

Why should Bertrand Russell, grandson of Lord John Russell, godson of John Stuart Mill, and deeply committed member of the Russell family branch of the Black Guelph families of Britain, ostensibly dedicate his adult life to ,"radicalism"? Russell had no emotional difficulty in opposing capitalism, because his class, his family have always been and remain perfervidly anticapitalist. They are "feudal" oligarchs in the deepest parts of their being, they are Black Guelph in the most evil connotations of that factional commitment. They are determined to destroy capitalism, and all other expressions of humanist policy, in order to bring back the "feudal" utopia for the lasting benefit of their families' posterity. Bertrand Russell rolled for decades in the slime of Dionysian anticapitalist cults, because he was a dedicated, deeply dedicated enemy of the human species. He gave his life's work to the posterity of his evil, oligarchical class.

It is only as one understands the Black Guelph in those terms of reference, that one comprehends how and why they fall so frequently into wild, masturbational fits in admiration of Maoist China. Granted, the late foreign Minister Chou En Lai had been a British agent since 1919-- yet, why their euphoria over Maoist China? It is the antihumanist, "labor-intensive" bucolic obscenity of Maoist

China which arouses their orgasms. It is the "feudal" oligarchy's zeal to restore the cult of Dionysus as the mythology of a mass of plebeians reduced to bucolic moral imbecility of human-manure tossing, instead of modern agricultural methods, which arouses their passions.

Conversely, whenever one notes this or that ostensible "conservative" political spokesman in Western Europe or North America making an obscene public spectacle of himself in admiration of Maoist China, the persistence of such episodes is a "litmus-test" certifying that conservative to be a British intelligence services' agent, a mercenary of the Black Guelph oligarchy centered in the British monarchy. A similar point is applicable to the case of those who rhapsodize over the memory of N. Bukharin in the Soviet Union.

This connection of the British monarchy, Black Guelph oligarchy, and British intelligence services to the "Persian model" is not simply an imitation resurrected through aid of Oxford and Cambridge scholars. The connection of today's Black Guelph oligarchy to the ancient Macedonian court and Ptolemaic Egypt is direct-- granting the point that in places, the continuing road winds somewhat. The continuity of the doctrines of Aristotle throughout the centuries into the policies and methods of the "neo-Aristotelians" of British empiricism, of pragmatism, is a direct continuity of antihumanist bestiality leading into the British intelligence services of the present date.

THE CASE OF ALEXANDER THE GREAT

To return to the fourth century BC, Alexander came out of exile to seize the throne of Macedon, bringing with and after him his close collaborators. Alexander was a committed follower of Plato, advised by leading representatives of Plato's Academy, and totally opposed to the "Persian model" policies of his father's court. His enthronement was, in consequence, a coup d'etat of Plato's faction against what we would term today the Aristotelian policies and faction of the Macedonian court.

This point was not overlooked by the Persians. A general mobilization was prepared by Philip of Macedon's erstwhile patrons, the Persian forces, preparatory to crushing Alexander. Alexander reacted decisively. Abandoning all vacillation or "Maginot Line" alternatives, he crossed to Anatolia, where an army of 25,000 foot and 5,000 horse awaited his command--resolved to defend his kingdom by defeating the Persian enemy before the enemy was adequately deployed for such enterprises as attacking Macedon itself.[15]

His first political act of that campaign was to restore the humanist constitutions of the Ionian city-states. Once he had completed the work of digging the Persian satrap's forces out of Miletus, that city became a leading force of his new Asia Minor base. The other, sweeping reforms he instituted in western Anatolia are exemplary of his Platonic policies.

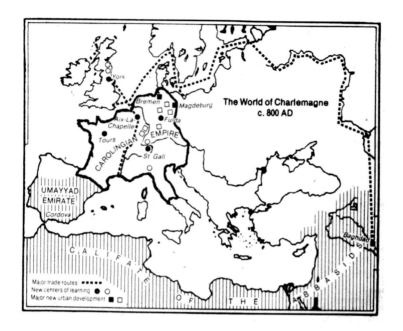

HUMANIST CITY-BUILDERS OF MEDIEVAL EUROPE AND ISLAM

As a result of collaboration of humanist networks stretching from Persia to northern England and Ireland, the Middle Ages produced fundamental advances in human civilization which were the basis for the European Renaissance.

The city-building policies of Charlemagne were the product of organizing by Irish and Anglo-Saxon Augustinian networks, and trading and diplomatic links with the humanist Abbasid Caliphate of Baghdad.

A key formulator of Charlemagne's policies was Alcuin of York, the master of Charlemagne's Palace school: Alcuin's and related institutions produced the leading intellectual figures of the next generation.

The World of Otto I
c. 1000 AD

Major trade routes
New centers of learning
Major new urban development

Otto I revived Charlemagne's policies in the 10th century, in close alliance with Spain's Abdul Rahman III.   Otto launched a major Christianizing-colonizing thrust to the east, expanding trade with Constantinople and points to the north and east. His reign coincided with the Ismaili humanists' establishment of Cairo as the capital of the new Fatimid Caliphate.

Otto and his successors' "Drive to the East" was continued in the 12th century by Henry the Lion, Duke of Saxony and Bavaria, while Emperor Frederick Barbarossa implemented the "Great Design" of building a model humanist state in the center of Western Europe. These impulses were reinforced by the circulation of the works of the Persian humanist Ibn Sina in Europe.

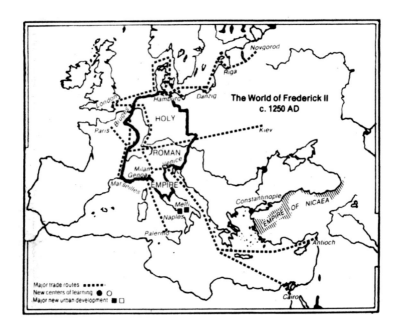

The World of Frederick II
c. 1250 AD

Major trade routes
New centers of learning
Major new urban development

The Holy Roman Empire reached its
zenith under the Hohenstaufen emperor
Frederick II. a leader of a humanist alliance
which included al-Kamil of Cairo, and which
engineered the rise of the Paleologue dynasty
in Constantinople. Frederick II himself
founded the first state-run university in Europe
at Naples in 1224. In 1226 he assigned the
Teutonic Order and its Grand Master, Hermann
von Salza, responsibility for development of
Prussia, helping to lay the foundations for the
later Hanseatic League.

SECRETS

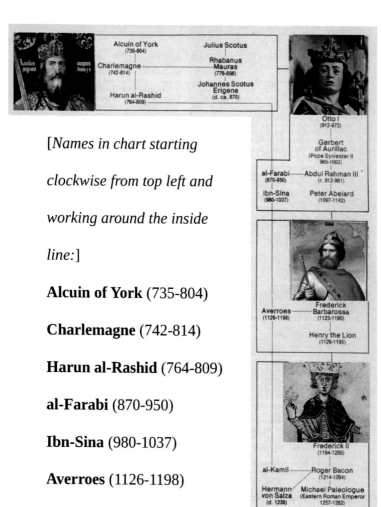

[*Names in chart starting clockwise from top left and working around the inside line:*]

Alcuin of York (735-804)

Charlemagne (742-814)

Harun al-Rashid (764-809)

al-Farabi (870-950)

Ibn-Sina (980-1037)

Averroes (1126-1198)

al-Kamil

Hermann von Salza (d. 1239)

[The Outside Line:]

Julius Scotus

Rhabanus Mauras (776-856)

Johannes Scotus Erigena (d. ca. 870)

Otto I (912-973)

Gerbert of Aurillac (Pope Sylvester II 965-1003)

Abdul Rahman III (r. 912-961)

Peter Abelard (1097-1142)

Frederick Barbarossa (1123-1190)

Henry the Lion (1129-1195)

Frederick II (1194-1250)

Roger Bacon (1214-1294)

Michael Paleologue (Eastern Roman Emperor 1257-1282)

After defeating the Persian forces in the battle of Issus (the battle for the Cilician gates), he rejected the Persian offer of the terms previously extended to Philip--the empire west of the Euphrates--also rejecting 10,000 talents and a Persian princess. He moved to besiege Tyre, an undertaking which succeeded through the offer of and negotiation of an alliance with the city of Sidon. The revolt of the Greek sections of the Persian fleet, and now the support of the revolting Phoenician fleet decided the issue in the eastern Mediterranean waters. The priests of Amon in Egypt staged an Egyptian revolt against the local Persian satrap, and negotiated what circumstances show to have been a city-building-policy alliance with the priests of

Amon--certifying this by ordering the opening of the canal from the Nile to the Red Sea.

Humanist, city-builder policies were Alexander's policies up to the point of his death at the hands of Aristotle's assassins. His policy was to develop Babylon as a center of world humanist culture and world trade, to dredge the Euphrates to Babylon, to build roads linking Babylon to the Mediterranean, and to develop education programs modeled on the Academy throughout the empire. There is recorded no policy like it known until the conscious commercial development policy of the Salian emperors of the eleventh century.

After his death and the division of his empire among the generals, (principally) his enemies, humanist policies were nonetheless reestablished at Athens--until the Ptolemies brought the Roman legions into Greece. With that event, and with the defeat of the humanist faction of the brothers Gracchi, the Apollo-ridden evil that was Rome degenerated rapidly into the imperial form. It is upon the latter, the protofascist Pax Romana, that the post-1660 Restoration British Black Guelph faction modeled its eighteenth century-adopted policy of Pax Britannica--or. rightly named, Pox Britannica. Behind mouthings of adoration of British agents-of-influence Metternich and Bismarck, it is the Pox Britannica to which British agent-of-influence Henry Kissinger is dedicated.

The legacy of Plato and Aristotle reemerged in the Hellenic world in and through the influence of the rise of Christianity as the fascist economic order that was imperial Rome underwent its lawful internal decay and weakening of its authority.[17]   It is not irrelevant that Christian humanism made no significant headway among the Latins themselves, but only enslaved Hellenic strata in Italy, and otherwise first in the Hellenic regions, extending to the barbarians. The indigenous population of Italy was too morally depraved by Roman culture.

Christianity lawfully lost its vitality in the Eastern Empire as it became a state religion during the post Constantine period. Cutting through fascinating details of the matter, the Aristotelian policy of coopting and syncretizing religious beliefs into forms suitable to serve as state cults was the root of the weakening. In the combined decay of Byzantium and of the episcopal Christianity attached to the Byzantine state, the germs of Platonic-Neoplatonic influence provided the environmental influence for the rise of the Prophet Muhammad, and the subsequent rise of the Ismaili humanist faction within Islam. The establishment of the cities of Baghdad, Sammara and Fatimid Cairo are cases of Ismaili-promoted new cities, continuing the policies of the ancient city-builder faction. The new cities developed in Persia also belong to the same category.

The transmission of civilization from Ismaili Islam to relatively barbaric Europe becomes most notable in the time of Charlemagne, and the circumstance of Charlemagne's liaison with his contemporary, Caliph Harun al-Rashid of Baghdad. From that point, a fight was joined in Europe between the Aristotelians (the monetarist banker-linked forces attempting, and often succeeding, in controlling the papacy) and the humanist currents.

Some of these Roman banking families were Jewish, bankers speculating in Roman real estate and engaged in control of a significant part of Mediterranean trade through correspondent connections with banking families as distant as Baghdad.

Historically the most important of such Jewish banking families of Rome was the Pierleoni.[18] Emulating another Roman Jewish banking family which had "converted" earlier to Christianity, to successfully benefit from the financial advantages of the papacy, the Pierleoni "converted" with the same purpose in view. One member of the family, styling himself Pope Gregory VI, took the direct route to his goal, buying the papacy from an incumbent pope. That sordid arrangement was nullified by intervention of the German emperor, and ex-Gregory VI and his heir Hildebrand, later Pope Gregory VII, were hustled off into exile.

This occurred during the eleventh century, and is no quaint element of church history but the focus of a chain of events which shaped the course of history over the following centuries, until the culmination of this policy in the mid-fourteenth century Black Death's killing of about half the existing population of central Europe. To follow events from 1045 AD to 1453 AD in the Mediterranean one must move one's attention constantly back and forth along the map from Rome to as far eastward as Mongolia. All the principal elements of history over that period are directly linked.

The period from Charlemagne through the Hohenstaufen produced and put into widespread use new scientific, industrial, and agricultural techniques which went significantly beyond the greatest achievements of Antiquity. The importance and widespread diffusion of medieval scientific culture is reflected in this illuminated manuscript drawing of the Almighty as an architect-engineer.

From approximately 1045 AD, Hildebrand, later Pope Gregory VII, was shaping European history for the worst. Hildebrand's immediate principal allies were Lotharingen, Matilda of Tuscany, the Guelphs allied to Maltilda, and the rich, corrupt Cluniac monastic order in France. Hildebrand's adversaries were the empire itself, the independent bishops and other clergy of the Church, and the humanist forces generally.

Three principal operations of that period were decisive in enabling Hildebrand to seize the Papacy. First, the Norman conquest of Saxon England and the associated project for the Norman conquest of Sicily. Second, the murder of three popes, two by Aristotelian methods within twenty-three days of one another, by Hildebrand's family's associates, a family then, among other functions, providing catering services to the papacy. Third, the alliance with the Seljuk Turkish mercenaries to attempt to crush the last bastions of Ismaili influence within Islam.

Through Hildebrand's securing the papacy, he, as Pope Gregory VII, instituted a series of what are euphemistically termed "reforms," which like many reputed reforms, were efficiently dedicated to institutionalizing a more hideous corruption than the reforms were reputed to have remedied.

First, the Norman conquest of Saxon England.

Saxon England was a far more civilized place in 1065 than it became again for a long time after the monstrous looting of the population by the Normans. It was the northern base of the Great Design of the German emperors, the northern point of trade routes running into

Venice and up across the mountain passes of Switzerland and Austria into the course of the Rhine and its tributaries. From the Black Sea, up the Danube, another channel of trade moved northward, joining with the Rhine tributaries. To the West, the Rhone and the Seine provided another axis of north-south trade, branching into the Meuse. At the intersection of the headwaters of these French rivers, in the vicinity of Aachen (Aix-la-Chapelle) down to the present Swiss border along the Rhine, east-west routes of trade joined. The Weser and the Elbe had emerging similar functions. From the rich south of France. in the Languedoc of the Albigensian developments, from Toulouse, along the Garonne to the port of Bordeaux, another key route linked the Mediterranean to the Saxon kingdom in the north.

The eleventh-century levels of per capita wealth and ratios of wealth in trade may appear tiny now, but those quantities in trade represented the sinews of transmission of technological and scientific knowledge. They have been the portion of the social tissue in which economic growth and progress have been located over the ages.

Hildebrand and his co-conspirators undertook to begin breaking the power of the empire by attacking its ally in the north. With aid of the intelligence-service capabilities of the Cluniacs, they attacked the Saxons on three fronts simultaneously. They rallied traitorous forces within Saxon England. They deployed the Scandinavians in an invasion that was to deplete the strength of King Harald prior to the Battle of Hastings. They launched the Norman invasion as a crusade--in fact, the first crusade as such--with Church blessings of the banners of the invaders and Church rallying of the invading forces.

The highpoint of medieval humanist culture saw a wave of cathedral building throughout Europe (facing page). Consuming in toto more stone than was used to build the ancient Egyptian pyramids, these advanced engineering marvels were deliberately designed to display rays of sunlight, symbolizing for the congregation the "flight of reason"--a concept dating back to Plato, while at the same time their grandeur and splendor celebrated the power of the human reason which designed and built them. Shown here is the choir of the magnificent. 150 foot-high Cologne Cathedral, begun in 1248, toward the close of the reign of Frederick II.

The murdering of elected popes terrorized other candidates to the point that Hildebrand was able, with aid of other means, to determine the succession to the papacy, finally installing himself.

A faction of Baghdad bankers of that time were allies of the Pierleoni in the joint fight against humanism, against city-builder policies.[19] Through their control of Baghdad and other cities, and through the promotion of Seljuk mercenaries (initially brought from the vicinity of present-day Afghanistan), they held the native Islamic population essentially in suppression and had reduced Ismaili power in the region from Mesopotamia eastward almost to nonexistence. However, the Ismaili tradition and influence was still powerfully embedded in sections of the population (it was not to be uprooted until after the Mongol conquest).

The principal Ismaili figure whose influence the Baghdad bankers most feared was that of Ibn Sina (Avicenna). In the effort to eliminate Ibn Sina's (and other Ismaili) influence, the Baghdad bankers resorted to the Aristotelian method, the cult-of-Dionysus tactic. An evil figure of some demogogic skill, al-Ghazali, was promoted by these bankers and their Seljuk allies, organizing a "sansculotte" movement of lumpens and bedouins to "purify" Islam of reason with an orgy of murder, rape and book-burning. A study of the commentaries in Burton's unexpurgated 1001 Nights, added to the study of the use of the al-Ghazali "Sufi" movement, identifies the methods principally used to this day by British intelligence services in manipulating Arabs and their governments. The British intelligence services have operated a synthetic "Ismaili" sect since the end of the eighteenth century (out of Oxford and Cambridge) and have also operated, with greater emphasis, an international "Sunni" movement also run out of Oxford, Cambridge and Sussex universities, as well as the London School of Economics.

By crushing the extremes of humanist influence, and by strengthening the Normans as a battering-ram-force against humanism, the Guelph forces associated with the Pierleoni created the circumstances advantageous for defeating the humanist forces.

Gregory VII's "reforms" concentrated both on breaking the independent power of the Church's bishops (the real purpose of his celibacy rule), and institution of the Aristotelian hoax of "canon law."20 The essence of this arrangement was to make Christendom nominally helpless before the swindles deployed under protection of the papacy by the Roman and other Guelph-allied banking families, and to ally with the most bucolically imbecilic strata of the nobility against "encroachments" by a humanist, Great Design policy of development. The other cornerstone of Gregory VII's policy was the combined institution of the Inquisition and Crusade, although the latter was not formally put into effect until after his death.

By the close of the eleventh century, the Cluniacs were too blatantly corrupt to be credible as religious authorities. They were replaced by the Cistercians, with whom is associated one of the most evil men in European history, Bernard of Clairvaux, who developed the model on which Martin Luther's theology was based.

The humanist forces were defeated but not crushed. The continuity of the Neoplatonic current was fully maintained.  In the East, Hassan ben Saba raised a new kind of force able to deal with the brutal methods of the Seljuks and followers of al-Ghazali, establishing a countervailing Ismaili power in the Middle East which persisted until the Mongol conquest of the thirteenth century.[21] The Knights Templars and Knights Hospitalers were influenced by the Ismailis. Despite the monstrous crimes against humanity perpetrated by a corrupted papacy in the name of the Crusades, humanist power resurged in Europe, especially around the Hohenstaufen from Frederick Barbarossa to Frederick II. Alfonso the Wise of Toledo was a cousin of Frederick II.

In a concerted operation, the Guelph faction and its allies to the East broke the power of the humanists during the seventh decade of the thirteenth century, celebrating this with the launching of the Inquisition against the Jews.

The strategic key to the operation in Europe lay in Asia. The Mongol invasion was the key. Although there never existed a Mongol "horde"--the Mongol male population of that period, boys and men, never exceeded one million by generous estimate--the Byzantine methods of conquest (chiefly by treachery) employed by Genghis Khan did leave some hideous bloodbaths in their aftermath. The papacy had had a liaison with the Mongol leaders since the twelfth century, contributing at least one church in

Mongolia at so early a date. It was the papacy which organized the Mongol invasion.

Hassan ben Saba, who had one of the best intelligence and intelligence-evaluations networks in all history to date, foresaw the shape of things being arranged, correctly assessed Genghis Khan's potentials, and dispatched forty assassins into Mongolia in a regrettably unsuccessful effort to shorten Genghis Khan's career.[22] The crushing of the economy to the East by the Mongol advance had the expected effects on Mediterranean trade, creating the circumstances in which the Templars were crushed by Philip le Bel of France, Alfonso the Wise overthrown in Spain, and Frederick II's power ended in Italy.

The thirteenth century was the period of rise of the Aristotelian faction as such within the Church. Previously, the most important intellectual influence in Europe had been that of Ibn Sina. Although Averroes of Toledo was not a consistent representative of Ibn Sina's work, Averroes (Ibn Rushd) was an Ismaili. It was he who had rebutted al-Ghazali's *The Destruction*, the  irrationalist attack on Ibn Sina, with his own *The Destruction of the Destruction*. (The Turks replied to Ibn Rushd with a book entitled, *The Destruction of the Destruction of the Destruction*). This Ismaili influence reached Europe not only by way of the Toledo school, but through Sicily and Venice, especially under the encouragement of Frederick II. All of the intellectual

leaders of Europe in philosophy and science during the
thirteenth century were chiefly influenced by the Ismailis.
England's Roger Bacon, for example, who died in prison at
the hands of the Dominicans under the Inquisition, is a
notable representative of Ibn Sina's influence. To combat
the humanist influence associated with Ibn Sina (Avicenna)
the Dominican order was deployed to lead the Inquisition,
turning to Aristotle as the Church's then-adopted official
philosopher, and following the policy adopted by Thomas
Aquinas in his irresponsible writings in criticizing the anti-
Aristotelian Ibn Sina as an erring "commentator" upon
Aristotle. The entire Aristotelian business was a hoax, as
Thomas Aquinas sadly suspected toward the close of his
own life.[23] During the fifteenth century, the documents
were studied which fully proved the whole Aristotelian
business a hoax, as well as the concoction known as "canon
law."

As a consequence of the triumph of the Guelph
faction with aid of Aristotle, the Guelph bankers enjoyed an
orgy   of   debt-pyramiding.   The   Jews--unwanted
competition--were driven off, as in England, as a side effect
of monarch's receipt of loans from the Bardi, Peruzzi and
other leading Guelph bankers. The pyramiding of the debts
of Europe's monarchs and other potentates led to an early
form of Schachtian "fiscal austerity." The labor on the
estates   was   intensified   and   estates   significantly
depopulated, as a means of producing a short-term increase
in debt-service payments capability. In the depletion and
mass vagabondage these austerity measures produced, the
population of central Europe was turned into a forcing-

culture for epidemic disease--half of the population was wiped out during the middle of the century.

The circumstances of the Black Death were also the circumstances of widespread repudiation of unpayable debts. This weakening of the power of the Guelph bankers and Guelph faction provided the opportunity for a resurgence of the humanist renaissance, this time in the form of the Renaissance of the fifteenth century. The Conciliar movement drastically reformed the papacy--and was then sent its way. This development in central Europe was reenforced by the rule of the humanist Paleologues in Byzantium. The long lived Georgios Gemistos Plethon, one of the greatest intellects of European history, brought to Italy from Byzantium the large bulk of the writings of Plato and other relevant materials on which European knowledge of Plato depends principally to the present date.[24]

This process of humanist progress was attacked by the Black Guelph in the traditional way--from the east. The Guelph families of Rome, in alliance with the patriarch of the Greek Orthodox Church, organized the fall of Constantinople into the hands of the Turk, Muhammad II, "The Conquerer."[25]

The key to the operation was the adoption of Aristotle as the official philosopher of the Eastern Church by the patriarch, a point underlined by the excommunication of Plethon as a Platonic. This measure, which isolated the Paleologues from aid by the Greek population, was decisive. When Constantinople was attacked, it was defended only by four thousand Genoese and a mere two thousand Greek militia. On the Turkish side, Muhammad II had siege cannon, *a technology supplied to him by the Guelph families of Rome!* At the same time, the Guelph deployed operations throughout key points in Europe, tying up Europeans in these affairs to the point that no adequate aid could be dispatched to Constantinople.[26]

This Black Guelph alliance with the Turks in the East was supplemented by an operation in the West, in Spain, the activation of the Reconquista and Inquisition under the leadership of the evil Ferdinand of Aragon and Castile, consort of Isabella. It is consistent with the character of Ferdinand that he, grandson of a Jew, launched the Inquisition against the Jews of Spain. Even before the Fugger-bought accession of Charles V Hapsburg to the throne of the Holy Roman Empire, the Guelph bankers of Italy and their client Ferdinand began to perform a crucial role in the destruction of the culture of the western region of the Mediterranean, including a growing evil role in Italy.

Although the Spanish infantry continued to play a potent role in Europe until its decisive defeat of 1653, Ferdinand created those institutions in Spain which lawfully degraded Spain from a major power into an impoverished "Third World" nation of the looted Iberian peninsula.

Ferdinand's role was to increase the dominance of the bucolic-imbecilic rural aristocracy of the *Reconquista* at the expense of the urban and cultured strata of Spain, using the Inquisition and the *limpieza de sangre* (purity of blood) as the principal instruments of this social program. It was his policies which shaped the later Spanish genocide in the Americas. (During approximately half a century during the later, sixteenth century, Spanish methods reduced the population of present-day Mexico from over twenty millions to less than two millions.)

The victory of the Guelph faction in the late thirteenth century and the consequent looting of the European population's means of existence led directly to the 14th century Black Death. The demoralization and bestiality imposed upon the European population-- particularly relative to the "Golden Age" of the Salians and Hohenstaufen that preceded it is expressed in this Florentine fresco, completed shortly after the Black Death.

However, it was not until after 1470, notably beginning the 1490s, that the consequences of the fall of Constantinople and Ferdinand's Spanish policies began to have disastrous effects. The Medici family, intimate collaborators of Plethon, established the Platonic Academy (e.g., of Marsilio Ficino) in Florence and spread Platonism throughout Europe. Plethon did more than bring Platonic scholarship to Western Europe. He was the author of a remarkable policy-formulation, proposed as a policy for defending Byzantium against the Turks, which incorporates every principal feature of modern capitalist policy for both industrial and agricultural growth, far in advance of anything Adam Smith, David Ricardo or their successors even understood. Who in Europe knew directly the contents of this remarkable document is not determined at this point, but the subsequent policies of France's Louis XI and the Dudleys of Tudor England show the same general policy-thrust.

Louis XI, as noted before, established modern France from the wreckage and pieces it had been over the preceding centuries, simultaneously multiplying not only the total wealth of the nation, but the per capita production of wealth. Through the faction of Navarre, and such *politiques* as Richelieu, Mazarin, Colbert, and their eighteenth century successors Vergennes, Turgot, and Brissot, French industrial-capitalist development was established. Through the humanist faction around the Tudors and the later Commonwealth Party of John Milton et al., industrial capitalism was also established in England beyond the ability of the post-1660 monarchical forces to undo this accomplishment.

GIORDANO BRUNO

The most important thinker of the fifteenth century was Cardinal Nicholas of Cusa (1401-1464), the first known thinker (possibly excepting Abelard) to fully replicate the conception of the "necessary existent" earlier developed in the *Metaphysics* of Ibn Sina. Nicholas was a universal mind, noted both for his political science contributions, such as the relatively early *Concordantia Catholica*, and his devastating attacks on Aristotle in the course of rigorously setting forth the method later employed by the greatest scientific thinkers of Europe through Gottfried W. Leibniz.

The most important direct intellectual successor of Cusa was the sixteenth century Giordano Bruno, burned at the stake by allied Guelph Catholic and Protestant officials for purely political reasons in 1600. As a result of the widespread destruction and suppression of Bruno's writings, and the terror his imprisonment and death effected among so many of his allies--including Galileo--it remains an open question whether we shall ever be able to reconstruct the full record of his power and influence in Europe during the last decades of the sixteenth century. So feared was Bruno that even the transcript of his trial was suppressed. What is known to date identifies him as one of the greatest intellects and most effective political personalities in European history.

It is known that Bruno established a network of organizations throughout Europe, and the chief parts of his work in England and France are known, especially his English work. The Dudleys, Sir Philip Sidney, and Christopher Marlowe were among his closest collaborators in England, and the princes of the House of Navarre his closest collaborators in France. It is also known that most extant Shakespeare scholarship is absurd, on the basis of the evidence turned up by focusing on Bruno's work in England.[28] It is relevant to all these points that Christopher Marlowe wrote "Doctor Faustus" in behalf of an effort to rescue Bruno from the Guelph Inquisition, and that English Tudor poetry, drama and music were based on the Platonic dialogue as a method, a matter in which Bruno's influence was direct and potent.

Bruno of the late sixteenth century is the key, common link for all humanist networks of the seventeenth century. As such, he is the dominant figure of that period, although one cannot now--and may never be certain-- determine what proportion of influence he directly contributed among all the influences intersecting his organizing and related efforts.[27]

In England, more broadly than just among those figures cited, his orbit was known as the "Italians," a circle to which William Shakespeare was junior, intersecting the work of John Dee, the activities of the teacher of the well-tempered system in England, John Bull, and the circles of the scientist William Gilbert, the discoverer of the first principles of magnetism--among other achievements,

Directly opposite to Bruno and his allies in England was the evil Cecil, and Cecil's appendage, the evil Francis Bacon. Elizabeth I vacillated, balancing, "neither wholly good nor wholly bad," between the Dudley-centered humanists and the Black Guelph faction of the Cecils. After the wretched Essex affair, the balance was tilted badly. With the accession of the wretched Stuart, James I, and James's Chancellor of the Exchequer, Francis Bacon, an inquisition was launched against the humanists, the English economy was set back, and the circumstances leading to the belated beheading of Charles I set into motion.

AMERICA VERSUS BRITAIN

The Erasmian Thomas More's *Utopia* was the poorest among the outlines of a project adopted by European humanists, notably sixteenth century English humanist leaders such as the Dudleys. The difficulties of establishing a humanist republic of viability under the encumbrance of deeply entrenched Guelphish institutions prompted thought of the ancient policies of the classic humanist city-builders. Go to the Americas, taking some of the best of the European humanists, and build a humanist society there by bringing modern technology to the natives. Use this as a base for building a humanist world order.[29]

This project was more vigorously pursued in the ebb of Elizabeth's reign and the hideousness of the Stuarts. The Massachusetts Bay Colony, Penn's Pennsylvania, Rhode Island, Connecticut, were leading elements of a general effort by the Commonwealth Party to launch such humanist colonizing projects during the seventeenth century. So, a selection of the best humanist minds of Europe and their predominantly literate supporters established those colonies. (Consequently, during the last half of the eighteenth century the literacy rate and social-productivity of the Americans was more than double that of Britain.)

In effect. the American Revolution was a civil war between the humanist and Guelph factions within British culture. It was a direct continuation of the civil war in seventeenth century England, and, was seen rightly as a civil war by those American leaders, typified by Paine, who sought to extend the American Revolution into England itself. By the close of the eighteenth century, there was an unbridgeable gulf between the leading American humanists and the ruling British empiricists.

As is generally known, the success of the American Revolution was secured, strategically, through the aid of the League of Armed Neutrality as well as French direct aid. The French aid was the center of this. The point of the matter is not that Benjamin Franklin secured French aid, but that Franklin was the leading American representative of the Commonwealth Party faction throughout the world, the heir of Penn, Milton, and others. The French humanists, for their part, were essentially *Colbertistes*, the historical allies of the English Commonwealth Party faction. Moreover, this alliance between Commonwealth Party and Colbertistes was a continuation of the alliance between the Tudor humanists of England and the House of Navarre from the fifteenth century, with roots going back to the time of Louis XI. The key eighteenth century figure to be added into the account is Gottfried Leibniz, the last universal mind of old Europe.

Against the humanists of the eighteenth century was arrayed the most evil machine ever developed, the Black Guelph ruling elite of Britain.

In the aftermath of the victory of the commonwealth, the Black Guelph oligarchical families of

Britain had either squatted sullenly in Britain, or had fled to the continent, the core to Holland. In exile, the leaders of this faction drew upon the resources of their allies throughout Europe, determined to build a policy and machine which would ensure their power forever, if --as they were determined--they could once again ensconce themselves in power in Britain.

Brooding in exile, these forces--typified by Hobbes, Francis Bacon's former secretary, and John Locke--worked out their master plan for dealing with the Platonic-Neoplatonic influence they hated and feared. Francis Bacon was their point of departure, and Aristotle their principal guide. They emulated Aristotle with a vengeance, hoping to replicate what they saw as Aristotle's victory over Plato's Academy. In the course of this they studied, attempted to master, and also to suppress from public knowledge the skills of their Neoplatonic enemies.

This development went through a second phase during the last decades of the eighteenth century. The defeat of Britain by the American Revolution and League of Armed Neutrality was a crisis for Britain, a crisis which led to the fore the circles of Lord Shelburne, Shelburne's protege William Pitt the Younger, and Shelburne's master of dirty work, Jeremy Bentham.

This crew, using Swiss and French agents under London's direction, wrecked French credit (Necker), mobilized the slum population (sansculottes) as an initial wrecking force (Orleans's staging of the storming of the Bastille, etc.), and then launched their trained agents Danton and Marat to set in motion the Jacobin Terror, launching the latter from inside the faction of Necker

American Civil War: A Global Conflict

The American Civil War was only one aspect of a global deployment of British-centered monetarists to complete the work begun when the Treaty of Vienna ratified monetarist hegemony over continental Europe. The Confederacy was a British project to dismember the United States. At the same time, the British dispatched Napoleon III of France to invade Mexico, in a campaign to stamp out humanist influences in Latin America which were centered around Mexican President Benito Juarez. British tool Bismarck was being groomed to help carve up Russia, and a fourth battleground was Japan, where a faction based on the economic theories of Americans Hamilton and Henry Carey battled a British-backed "Rothschild" faction.

The British plans were defeated by a triad of leaders who drew explicitly on the work of Alexander Hamilton and the American founding fathers as their point of reference: President Lincoln, Russia's Czar Alexander II, and Juarez. The Czar's efforts were particularly significant for the eventual success of the Union. During 1862, the British and their French stooges were deterred from entering the war on the side of the Confederacy only by the Czar's public expressions of support for the Union which included the dispatch of Russian fleets to New York and San Francisco to counter the British threat, as well as conveying messages that a British intervention against the United States would be regarded as a casus belli *by Russia.*

protege and dupe Robespierre. The success of the Shelburne gang in reducing continental Europe into a war-ruin until 1814, and the successful establishment of the bucolic imbecility, the Holy Alliance, as an instrument for paying dividends on debts to the City of London, established the Shelburne gang and its tradition as the ruling force in and around the British monarchy to the present date.

The poor fools, with. a "different perception" of history, are the lawful, helpless prey of that mob attached to the British monarchy. Believing the historical and other mythologies concocted for such credulous fools as themselves, the British can perform the same tired old Aristotelian swindles upon them yet another time, without facing an effective defense, and without the victims even then awakening to the reality of what has been done to them.

Notes

l.   Criton Zoakos, "Aristotle and the Craft of Intelligence," *New Solidarity,* Vol. VIII, Nos. 99, 100 (Feb. 24 and 28, 1978). See the policy statement authored by Persian-Macedonian agent Isocrates, of the Athenian school of rhetoric. The record of the "check stubs" of payments to agent Demosthenes by the Persian-Macedonian forces still exists.

2.   Criton Zoakos, "Aristotle and the Craft of Intelligence."

3.   Criton Zoakos et al. Also (cf. Gregory, "Aristotle and the Cult of Dionysus." [Unpublished: Wiesbaden, 1978]) the role of Alcibiades in pushing the Magna

Grecia campaign in the form and at the time most expedient for the troubled Persians.

4. Gregory, "Aristotle and the Cult of Dionysus."

5. Cf. Paul Arnest, "From Babylon to Jerusalem," p. 64.

6. Livy is the standard source on this. See the commentaries on Livy by Machiavelli. On the role of the Ptolemies in the Romans' campaign against Greece, see Gregory.

7. Cf. Linda Frommer, "How Pitt's, Jacobinism Wrecked the French Revolution," *New Solidarity*, Vol. VIII, No. 28 (June 3, 1977) and Vol. VIII, No. 29 (June 7, 1977) and David Goldman, "How the City of London Got Through the Revolutionary War Crisis," *New Solidarity*, Vol. VIII, No. 78 (Dec. 2, 1977) and Vol. VIII, No. 79 (Dec. 6, 1977) on the French Revolution. Lord Shelburne, allied to the Barings and the British East India company, used the circumstances of the 1783 Treaty of Paris to bring his circles into a dominant position within the British monarchy, putting William Pitt the Younger forward as the most visible accomplice of his circles. Adam Smith, Jeremy Bentham, the Mills, Thomas Malthus, (later) David Ricardo, and others were tools of this Shelburne centered reorganization of British intelligence. This was the predecessor phase for the later reorganization toward the close of the nineteenth century, in which the emergence of the Fabian Society and Lord Milner's networks were the most prominent feature--including the Rhodes Scholarship project for aiding the subverting of the United States by the British intelligence services.

Necker, who wrecked the French credit from within-- much like W. Michael Blumenthal and James R. Schlesinger wrecked the dollar for the British during 1977-78, was a part of the Geneva-centered circles of British intelligence. The Duke of Orleans was a British agent to the end. Danton and Marat were British-trained and British-coordinated agents-provocateurs, deployed from London to organize the Jacobin Terror. Robespierre was a protege and dupe of Necker's circles. And, so on and so forth.

8. Criton Zoakos, "Aristotle and the Craft of Intelligence."

9. On the Royal Society and Newton, cf. Carol White, "The Royal Society," *Fusion*, Vol. I, Nos. 3-4, Dec.-Jan. 1977-1978, pp. 44-53.

10. Criton Zoakos, "Aristotle and the Craft of Intelligence."

11. Criton Zoakos and Erini Levedi, "The Paleologue Dynasty as Instruments of the Hohenstaufen Grand Design" (Unpublished: New York, 1978). The Paleologues developed a humanist faction in Russia, reflecting the conceptions of statecraft associated with Georgios Gemistos Plethon. Ivan III's policies were derived from this work, as was the later campaign against the Aristotelian-oligarchical faction (e.g., the Boyars) by Ivan IV ("The Awesome").

12. Konstantin George, "The U.S.-Russian Entente That Saved the Union," to be published in *The Campaigner*, Vol. XI, No. 6 (July 1978).

13. Cf. Allen Salisbury, *The Civil War and the American System* (New York: Campaigner Publications, Inc., 1978).

14. *Ibid.* See also, *The Political Economy of the American Revolution* (New York: Campaigner Publications, Inc., 1977), passim.

15. Criton Zoakos, "Aristotle and the Craft of Intelligence."

16. Helga Zepp, Unpublished paper: Wiesbaden, 1978.

17. The characterization of the Roman Empire as economically fascist is no hyperbole. The fascism associated with Mussolini and Nazism are only varieties of states based upon Aristotelian policies of genocidal fiscal austerity in behalf of monetarist debt pyramids and in opposition to technologically vectored solutions to "depressions." It is significant that the fascist movements of Italy and Weimar Germany were products of the work of British intelligence networks, and that both Mussolini and Hitler were put in power on directives from London. Turning attention from the monetarist policies which essentially characterized Mussolini's and Hitler's policies, and focusing on the kind of social base created to support such a state machine, the "leftism" of Mussolini's followers and of most of the Nazis' SA base not accidentally compares in essentials with the Maoism and "environmentalism" of present-day North America and Western Europe. The sociology of those base forces is the elaboration of the doctrines of the Phrygian cult of Dionysus. To see Julius Caesar as a fascist, and to see his relationship to his lumpen social base in Rome in those terms, is not only admissible, but is the only efficient conceptual approach to understanding Caesar and the policies and unfolding history of the Roman Empire.

18. Information based on unpublished studies by Costas Kalimtgis, Steven Douglas, and others.

19. Judith Wyer, "A Humanist Perspective on Medieval Islam" (Unpublished: New York, 1978).

20. Kalimtgis, Douglas, et al.

21. Criton Zoakos, "The Order of the Assassins," Lecture: Chicago, April 17, 1978.

22. *Ibid.*

23. Criton Zoakos, "Ibn Sina and the Dawn of the Humanist Heritage," *The Campaigner*, Vol. X, No. 3 (July-August, 1977) pp. 10-43.

24. Zoakos and Levedi, "The Paleologue Dynasty."

25. *Ibid.*

26. *Ibid.* Zoakos secured much of this on the Byzantine phase of the matter through the works of Greek historians of the 1920s. These sources documented facts contrary to the mistaken views of the usual secondary sources concerning the role of Plethon in connection with the fifteenth century ecumenical negotiations.

27. This summary of the events surrounding Bruno is based in large part on the coordinated efforts of a number of researchers in Europe and North America. Work on the Ismailis by Criton Zoakos, Helga Zepp, Judith Wyer and others. Work on the Tudor period coordinated by Christopher White. Work on Bruno by specialists on both continents, work on Nicholas of Cusa by Helga Zepp and others. Work on Leibniz by Uwe Parpart, Carol, White, and others. A short biography of Bruno is

given by Nora Hamerman in her preface to the first English translation of Bruno's dialogue, "The Cabala of the Winged Horse, with the Addition of the Cyllenian Ass," in *The Campaigner*, Vol. XI. No. 2 (March 1978).

28. Bruno's short dramatic works provide a key to the work of Christopher Marlowe and others. Christopher White has been able to demonstrate the secrets of Elizabethan drama by a closely analyzed treatment of the immediate references embodied in Shakespeare's Hamlet. See Christopher White, "Shakespeare's Revenge," *New Solidarity*, Vol. IX, Nos. 3, 4, 5, 9, 11, March 10, 14, 17, 31 and April 7, 1978.

29. Christopher White, et al.

II. THE KEY TO HISTORY

The rigorous study of human history as a whole proceeds methodologically from a preliminary division of historiography into three sub-categories. Each of these three, overlapping categories is distinguished from the other two by a specific time-span of its principal, distinct applicability, and also by the distinctions among methods and materials of evidence peculiarly emphatic for each time-span.

The first is *history as such, the conscious history of the rise of Mediterranean and adjoining civilization* as developed from the starting point of literary evidence. This category begins as a continuity in approximately the eighth century BC.

The *second* category is *archaeological history*, whose span begins, varying with locale, approximately between eight and four thousand BC. Although some literary or proto literary records are obtained from parts of this part, the evidence employed is predominantly non-literary artifacts from the sites of urban centers. The methods developed in such work have been extended in application to agrarian and pastoral sites, and to earlier periods.

The *third* sub-category is the *paleontological history* of our species. This is currently believed to begin between two and three million years ago, during the Pleistocene.[5]

Beginning with the first category, history as such, the preliminary ordering of the account is produced through cross-checking literary records and of some other forms of other evidence, to produce the reconstructed annals of a period of culture in terms of such sources. The literary bits and pieces are thus assembled into a reasonably corroborated narrative account of notable events reported to have occurred at the indicated points of the calendar. This sort of narrative account is indispensable, but only preliminary to actual historiography. It does not represent in itself the essential quality of workmanship by which the historian is properly distinguished from the mere story-teller.

Historiography begins with informed distrust of literary source-documents from the periods studied. Surviving literary records must be approached with the assumption that such records either are or might probably be defective on several counts. The following illustrative listing of the kinds of probable defects adequately presents the point for this stage of the discussion.

First, narrative history begins as we have noted, with *surviving* literary records available to us. This includes not only ordinary literary records, but inscriptions on various monuments and so forth. This source-material as a whole has the obvious defect of not including documents which have not survived, some of which may be as significant as those prominent in the available collections. It also omits the literary materials not written, but which would be required if we were to possess testimony concerning all important transactions. There are, similarly, the monuments which were either destroyed--or not constructed--to the same effect. In all this, in most periods the portion of the population which left a literary record was small and selective.

Second, in addition to willful falsifications of fact in official and other source-documents, the rulership and internal ordering of societies has always centered to this time around sets of mythologies. Only special categories of records, created by special kinds of persons under special circumstances have the authority of candor, and still fewer of that same special class represent *efficient* candor for the professional historian's purposes. In general, the source-documents of history have not been designed on the basis of "objectivity." History has been recorded chiefly for the time and circumstances in which source-documents were written. What is said is usually intended to be credible by prevailing standards of that period. Usually, for a report to meet the contemporary requirements of credibility, it must not make itself incredible by offending prevailing mythologies entirely. It must, in most cases, appeal to credibility as some existing mythology of that time defines credibility. Surviving documents, even were they adequate as accounts of significant occurrences, could not reflect reality as the disciplined historian properly requires. They reflect, overall, principally a mixture of willful falsifications and adaptations to the mythologies of their place and time.

Third, apart from falsifications and mythologies, most of the authors of source-documents were incompetent to judge the events of their time, to determine why certain consequences ensued from this or that development, or

what was in fact important in determining the course of
events.

All these and related faults of source-documents and
related evidence, the historian must remedy. History merely
as given to us from sources does not yield a narrative to
which we can directly and competently address the
questions beginning with "Why?"

THE CASE OF BISMARCK

A further, principal problem of historiography, a
problem which few generally accredited historians have so
far comprehended in anything near adequacy, is the
impossibility of developing a competent account of an
isolated part of history in terms of materials available in
sources from such a specific locale and period. The case of
Bismarck illustrates the point.

Most of the textbook and related treatment of
Bismarck and of Germany during the last half of the
nineteenth century is almost useless for understanding the
"Why?" of the events of that period and region.

Bismarck's accession to the Prussian Chancellory
was in no respect chiefly a product of circumstances
internal either to Prussia itself or Germany as a whole.
Bismarck was conspicuously a cultivated protege of the
House of Rothschild, and ascended to the Chancellery
through notable interventions centered in London origins.
In all major respects, Bismarck was a British agent-of-
influence. He won the war with Austria (1866) because
London rigged the treasuries and the "radical" movements
of Europe to procure and secure that result. He won the

Bismarck (in white coat, right foreground) presides at the coronation of Kaiser Wilhelm I at the French palace of Versailles in 1871, the culmination of years of British efforts to "unify" Germany under Bismarck's nominal control.   The British had unleashed their puppet "Iron Chancellor" against the hapless Napoleon III in the preceding year's Franco-Prussian War to head off French impulses toward industrial-capitalist development.

Franco-Prussian war under London's auspices and pre-arrangements. It was the British oligarchy's preference that Germany be unified (in its main parts) under a Prussian monarchy and oligarchy being molded by London's influence into emulation of the British model.

Although one can point meaningfully to prominent, included features of the nineteenth century "concert of Europe" to account for the secondary aspects of London's

Prussian preference, the criteria by which those empirics were judged in London are not located in the nineteenth century, but in the millennial history of the "Persian model" policies of the Black Guelph faction.

London's Prussian policy is clearer when compared with London's policy concerning Napoleon III, its Mexican policy, and its policy for attempting to reconquer the United States.

The France of Napoleon III was notably a Saint Simonian sort of deformed humanist-republican impulse for industrial progress, contained within and overwhelmed by arrangements dominated more visibly by the "second emperor of France," Baron James Rothschild. To be more exact, former-British special gendarme Louis Bonaparte had been preferred by British influences, to the purpose of containing the republican impulses expressed in the events of 1848 and 1848's aftermath.

Thus, within limits, Napoleon III was for a time an interest of London's foreign policy. By 1866-1870 the time had arrived, in London's perception, for dumping Louis Napoleon.

In the broadest terms, the weakening of France's power on the continent of Europe had been the policy of the Guelph faction and that faction's Roman-banker predecessors since the time of Charlemagne. The pope who officiated at the imperial crowning of Charlemagne and Charlemagne recognized one another as principled adversaries, not notably on personal grounds, but in term's of the policies and interests they respectively represented and typified. It was not a conflict between the emperor and

Christian Church, but between Europe and the forces committed to the "Persian model," which latter at that point, and too frequently thereafter, controlled the papacy. This difference was expressed formally by Charlemagne's denunciation of the forgery known as "The Donation of Constantine," the forgery which purported to be the Emperor Constantine's decree placing secular rule of the Western Roman Empire under the authority of the bishop of Rome. France's position as the strongest of the civilized nations of western Europe represented to the Roman bankers controlling the papacy the key political force capable of undoing their efforts to perpetuate the policies of the cult of Apollo and its Stoic version under Christian titles.

The Scandinavian berserkers' invasion of France was the first of the principal developments which had weakened France to the advantage of the "Christian" agents of the cult of Apollo. The weakening of France had shifted the main political focus of opposition to Apollonian policies to the German Holy Roman emperor. However, without an alliance between Germany and France, subsequent history repeatedly demonstrated, the combination needed to defeat the Apollonian interest was usually lacking.

Guelph policies against France date efficiently from the founding of the Guelph faction during the eleventh century. The Guelph mobilization of the Norman Conquest of Saxon England created a Norman power in the north of France which, especially after Simon de Montfort's slaughter of the Albigensians, threatened, weakened and repeatedly almost destroyed France, until Louis XI

completed the work inaugurated around the figure of
Jeanne d'Arc.

Although Navarre was allied to the humanist Tudor
faction, and Cromwell's England to Mazarin's France,
France's English allies had always been the Guelphs'
enemies.

The model for British Guelph French policy from
1660 to the present date is the House of Orange's operation
against Colbert's France.   The House of Orange
undermined both the French Colbertistes and the Dutch
humanists (De Witt, Spinoza, et al.), by strengthening the
grip of the rural-aristocratic faction in Louis XIV's court,
and launching Louis XIV into his wars *against the House
of Orange*. In the course of that development, the humanist
forces in both England and France were then weakened
significantly, by Marlborough's campaigns in behalf of the
Dutch Hanoverian interest, and by the simultaneous
launching of the two financial bubbles, the South Sea Island
and Mississippi bubbles, in both England and France.

The same policy was applied, somewhat more
elaborately to post-1783 France. It must be borne in mind,
to understand Anglo-Dutch Black Guelph policy during
that period, that it had been the French-led League of
Armed Neutrality which had proven strategically decisive
in enabling the victory of the American Revolution. After
scrambling the post-1789 efforts of French humanists to
construct a French republic on the basis of the American
constitutional model and policies, London and its allies
undid the related impulses among the circles around
Carnot--through Napoleon I.

The murder of Dutch humanist Jan de Witt and his brother Cornelius at the hands of a hired mob in 1672, as depicted in a contemporary print by Romeyn de Hooghe. Allied with Spinoza and supporters of the English Commonwealth, the De Witts were murdered and their bodies mutilated by rioters paid with funds provided by the House of Orange and laundered through the Calvinist "alms"-giving charity network.

THE AMERICAN CONSPIRACY

	1550		1600	
Italy	Gioseffo Zarlino (1517-1590): Musical theorist and proponent of well-tempered scale. Teacher of Galileo's father.		Giordano Bruno (1548-1600): Leading international humanist organizer; scientist, philosopher, and author. Burned as a heretic by the Inquisition. ●	Galileo Galilei (1564-1642): Leading scientist and opponent of Aristotelianism. Correspondent of Kepler and William Gilbert; acquainted with Milton.
Scandinavia, Germany and Central Europe	Tycho Brahe (1546-1601): Danish astronomer; imperial mathematician in Bohemia.		Johannes Kepler (1571-1630): Initiates modern mathematical physics with his *Astronomia Nova* (1603); successor to Tycho Brahe in Bohemia. Friend and ally of Bruno. ●	Gustavus Adolphus (1594-1632): King of Sweden. Fought Hapsburgs in Thirty Years War; promoted commerce, industry, and education in Sweden.
France	Jean Bodin (1530-1596): *Politique* and architect of a unified France; linked to Gresham tendency in England.			Girard Desargues (1593-1662): Engineer, mathematician and architect; introduced Descartes to Richelieu. René Descartes (1596-1650): Humanist organizer, scientist and philosopher. Publishes humanist program. *A Discourse on Method.* 1637. ●
Low Countries		Jan van Olden Barneveldt (1547-1619): Dutch statesman; ally of the Tudors, connected with Grotius.	Simon Stevin (1548-1620): Scientist, mathematician, and engineer. Battled Aristotelianism; first introduced decimals into widespread usage. Jan Sweelinck (1562-1621): Organist and composer; influenced Bach.	Hugo Grotius (1583-1645): Humanist organizer and legal theoretician; formulated theory of international law based on natural law.
England	John Dee (1527-1608): Tudor intelligence officer, mathematician, scientist, and ally of Giordano Bruno.	Thomas Gresham (1519-1579): Tudor financier; promoted industrialization of England. Robert Dudley (1532-1588): Leading organizer against the Hapsburgs; sought to create an England-France-Netherlands axis.	Christopher Marlowe (1564-1603): Humanist playwright; ally and protege of Giordano Bruno. William Gilbert (1544-1603): Physician to Tudor Court; author of *De Magnete*, basic treatise on magnetism published in 1600.	John Bull (1562-1628): Physicist, composer and musical theorist. Attacked by Francis Bacon. William Shakespeare (1564-1619): Humanist playwright. Opposed Stuart takeover of English throne. William Harvey (1578-1657): Found path of circulation of the blood. 1628.
America				William Bradford (1590-1657): Pilgrim father; first governor of Plymouth Colony. Had connections to Leyden University. John Winthrop, Sr. (1588-1649): First governor of Massachusetts; leading opponent of James I.

The American Revolution was the product of more than two centuries of international humanist organizing. European humanists centered around Erasmus, Bruno and the English Tudors actively worked to develop the New World; the French Colbertistes saw the growth of America as support for their program to industrialize France; and the scientific and political conceptions generated by Leibniz's networks

1650	1700	1750

● Pictured beside

John Amos Comenius
(1592-1670): Educator based in Bohemia: associated with Hartlib and Milton: visited England during Commonwealth period. Friend of John Winthrop, Jr.

G. W. von Leibniz ●
(1646-1716): Humanist organizer: philosopher and scientist. Fought to revive "Grand Design" in Europe. Elaborated conception of the unity of natural and human law.

Eugene of Savoy
(1663-1736): Fostered growth of humanist forces in Austria: correspondent of Leibniz.

Cardinal Richelieu
(1602-1661): Forged modern French nation, opponent of Hapsburg designs in Central Europe: linked to Descartes.

Cardinal Mazarin
(1602-1661): Successor to Richelieu, ally of Cromwell and De Witt: architect of League of the Rhine, 1658.

Jean-Baptiste Colbert
(1619-1683): French statesman, centralized nation's finances and developed national industrialization program. Patron of science and the arts. ●

Rembrandt van Rijn
(1606-1669): Dutch painter, innovator in printmaking techniques and one of history's greatest portrait artists. Humanist ally of Huygens, Spinoza, De Witt. ●

Jan De Witt
(1625-1672): Dutch statesman, allied with Commonwealth against House of Orange, 1654. Murdered by monetarist mob, 1672.

Benedict Spinoza
(1632-1677): Humanist philosopher and political theorist: allied with De Witt. Formulated advanced ethical conception of individuals' responsibility to effect progress.

Christiaan Huygens
(1629-1695): Leading scientist: tutored Leibniz in mathematics. ●

John Milton
(1608-1674): Poet and political theoretician of the Commonwealth.

Oliver Cromwell ●
(1599-1658): Leader of Great Rebellion against the Stuarts, established English Commonwealth, 1649.

Samuel Hartlib
(1600-1662): Economist and educational reformer: active in England during Commonwealth period; friend and ally of Milton.

Robert Hooke
(1635-1703): Inventor and scientist: professor at Gresham College.

Benjamin Franklin
(1706-1790): Leading humanist organizer of 18th century: founded Junto in 1727: gained international renown for scientific work. Led American Revolution.

Thomas Dudley
(1576-1653): Four times governor of Massachusetts between 1634-1650; founder of Harvard College. Descendant of Robert Dudley.

Roger Williams
(1603-1685): Friend of Milton: opponent of Charles I. Founded Providence 1636: Rhode Island 1644.

John Winthrop, Jr.
(1606-1676): Governor of Massachusetts and founder of Connecticut. Scientist and correspondent of Milton, Hartlib, and Leyden arabists. **William Penn** (1644-1728): Founder of Pennsylvania, 1681.

Increase Mather
(1639-1723): Scholar scientist: colonial ambassador to England. President of Harvard College, and Minister at church attended by Franklin. Founded Philosophical Society.

James Logan
(1674-1751): Secretary to William Penn, 1699. Merchant, scientist: founder of humanist library in Philadelphia which was an organizing center for Franklin.

George Washington
(1732-1799): Leader of pro-industrial faction in the South: early collaborator of Franklin; commander of Colonial armies and first President of United States.

were rapidly circulated in the American colonies.

[Below are the descriptions from this chart. Descriptions are in columnar order starting from the top left.--ed.]

Gioseffo Zarlino (1517-1590): Musical theorist and proponent of well-tempered scale. Teacher of Galileo's father.

John Dee (1527-1608):   Tudor intelligence officer: mathematician, scientist, and ally of Giordano Bruno.

Tycho Brahe (1546-1601):   Danish astronomer;   imperial   mathematician   in Bohemia.

Jean Bodin (1530-1596):   *Politique* and architect of a unified France: linked to Gresham tendency in England.

Thomas Gresham (1519-1579):   Tudor financier: promoted   industrialization   of England.

Robert Dudley (1532-1588):   Leading organizer against the Hapsburgs; sought to create an England-France-Netherlands axis.

Giordano Bruno (1540-1600):   Leading international humanist organizer;   scientist, philosopher, and author. Burned as a heretic by the Inquisition.

Jan van Olden Barneveldt (1547-1619): Dutch statesman; ally of the Tudors, connected with Grotius.

Christopher Marlowe (1564-1603): Humanist playwright; ally and protege of Giordano Bruno.

William Gilbert (1544-1603):   Physician to Tudor Court; author of *De Magnete*, basic treatise on magnetism, published in 1600.

Galileo Galilei (1564-1642): Leading scientist and opponent of Aristotelianism. Correspondent of Kepler and William Gilbert; acquainted with Milton.

Johannes Kepler (1571-1630): Initiates modern mathematical physics with his *Astronomia Nova* (1603); successor to Tycho Brahe in Bohemia. Friend and ally of Bruno.

Simon Stevin (1548-1620): Scientist, mathematician, and engineer. Battled Aristotelianism; first introduced decimals into widespread usage.

Jan Sweelinck (1562-1621): Organist and composer; influenced Bach.

John Bull (1562-1628): Physicist, composer, and musical theorist. Attacked by Francis Bacon.

William Shakespeare (1564-1619): Humanist playwright. Opposed Stuart takeover of English throne.

Gustavus Adolphus (1594-1632): King of Sweden. Fought Hapsburgs in Thirty Years War; promoted commerce, industry, and education in Sweden.

Girard Desargues (1593-1662): Engineer, mathematician and architect; introduced Descartes to Richelieu.

Rene Descartes (1596-1650): Humanist organizer, scientist, and philosopher. Publishes

humanist program, *A Discourse on Method,*
1637.

Hugo Grotius (1583-1645):   Humanist
organizer and legal theoretician; formulated
theory of international law based on natural
law.

William Harvey (1578-1657):   Found path of
circulation of the blood, 1628.

William Bradford (1590-1657):   Pilgrim
father; first governor of Plymouth Colony. Had
connections to Leyden University.

John Winthrop, Sr. (1588-1649):   First
governor of Massachusetts; leading opponent of
James I.

John Amos Comenius (1592-1670):   Educator
based in Bohemia; associated with Hartlib and
Milton; visited England during Commonwealth
period.   Friend of John Winthrop, Jr.

Cardinal Richelieu (1602-1661):   Forged
modern French nation; opponent of Hapsburg
designs in Central Europe; linked to Descartes.

Thomas Dudley (1576-1653):   Four times
governor of Massachusetts between 1634-1650;
founder of Harvard College.   Descendant of
Robert Dudley.

Cardinal Mazarin (1602-1661): Successor to
Richelieu; ally of Cromwell and De Witt;
architect of League of the Rhine, 1658.

Rembrandt van Rijn (1606-1669): Dutch painter; innovator in printmaking techniques and one of history's greatest portrait artists. Humanist ally of Huygens, Spinoza, De Witt.

John Milton (1608-1674): Poet and political theoretician of the Commonwealth.

Oliver Cromwell (1599-1658): Leader of Great Rebellion against the Stuarts; established English Commonwealth, 1649.

Roger Williams (1603-1685): Friend of Milton, opponent of Charles I. Founded Providence, 1636; Rhode island, 1644.

Jan De Witt (1625-1672): Dutch statesman; allied with Commonwealth against House of Orange, 1654. Murdered by monetarist mob, 1672.

Samuel Hartlib (1600-1662): Economist and educational reformer; active in England during Commonwealth period; friend and ally of Milton.

John Winthrop, Jr. (1606-1676): Governor of Massachusetts and founder of Connecticut. Scientist and correspondent of Milton, Hartlib, and Leyden arabists.

William Penn (1644-1728): Founder of Pennsylvania, 1681.

G. W. von Leibniz (1646-1716): Humanist organizer, philosopher and scientist. Fought to revive "Grand Design" in Europe. Elaborated conception of the unity of natural and human law.

Jean-Baptiste Colbert (1619-1683): French statesman; centralized nation's finances and developed national industrialization program. Patron of science and the arts.

Benedict Spinoza (1632-1677): Humanist philosopher and political theorist; allied with De Witt. Formulated advanced ethical conception of individuals responsibility to effect progress.

Increase Mather (1639-1723): Scholar, scientist, colonial ambassador to England. President of Harvard College, and Minister at church attended by Franklin. Founded Philosophical Society.

Eugene of Savoy (1663-1736): Fostered growth of humanist forces in Austria; correspondent of Leibniz.

Christiaan Huygens (1629-1695): Leading scientist; tutored Liebniz in mathematics.

Robert Hooke (1635-1703): Inventor and scientist; professor at Gresham College.

James Logan (1674-1751): Secretary to William Penn, 1699. Merchant, scientist, founder of humanist library in Philadelphia which was an organizing center for Franklin.

Benjamin Franklin (1706-1790): Leading humanist organizer of 18th century; founded

Junto in1727; gained international renown for
scientific work. Led American Revolution.

George Washington (1732-1799): Leader of
pro-industrial faction in the South; early
collaborator of Franklin; commander of
Colonial armies and first President of United
States.

* * *

It must be noted, to appreciate British policy of that
period, that 1784-1812 England was objectively helpless
against the power of France. Despite the myths later
concocted for the misdirection of the credulous, France of
the last half of the eighteenth century was by far the major
and most progressive industrial power of the world--despite
the oligarchical yoke of serfdom persisting in French
agriculture. Only by inducing France to destroy itself on
the continent of Europe could Britain defeat France--and
also place all Europe under the British satrapy known as the
Holy Alliance. In addition to Anglo-Dutch agent
Talleyrand, and despite continued humanist tendencies
represented by Carnot, the Napoleonic regime was riddled
with Black-Guelphish ideologies, typified by the
oligarchical struttings of the Napoleonic elite and the
degrading influence of Roman law. Napoleon I, by
emulating the follies of Louis XIV, ultimately won the
Napoleonic wars for England.

The model of Napoleon I was parodied by the
British and their allies in fostering the judo tactic embodied
in Napoleon III.

What London feared, especially after its experience in the United States' Civil War, was the potential that French and German Rhineland industrial interests would ally programmatically with the emerging political labor movement of those nations, and set into motion an "American Revolution" on the continent of Europe. This potentiality London perceived to be the fatal weakness situated in the regime of Napoleon III, and so the basis in perception for the urgency of the humiliation of France by a Germany under Prussian rule.

Admittedly, in following that Prussian policy, London set into motion in Germany an industrial impulse echoing awkwardly the very impulse it had attempted to crush in France. However, this oversight of London's did not take important political form until after the ushering of Bismarck from the Chancellery.

The circumstances of 1866-1871 in Europe were determined by preceding developments in North America.

The "French faction" in the eighteenth century Spanish Borbon court had transmitted into the cultured circles of Latin America the echo of the "Great Design" policy which was the Greater Spain project. All the Spanish colonies were to be elevated in political status to form a transatlantic Spanish state, a state dedicated to scientific, technological and cultural progress. The defeat of this humanist faction in Spain by the rise of the British-linked Godoy, and the British puppet-status of Spain and Portugal throughout the nineteenth (into the twentieth) century, had left the active kernel of the Spanish humanists in the colonies.

Thus, one had, in the case of Mexico, the irony of an independent monarchy pushed forward by the British rulers of Spain, where the Mexican humanists still aspired to play their role in the Greater Spain project, the transatlantic republic.

Among the most fortunate of the Spanish colonies intellectually was Mexico, the nation in which the humanist influence was most deeply planted and solidly based in the intelligentsia. Here, a genuine civil war has been conducted down into the establishment of the modern Mexican constitution, the struggle between the humanist faction (e.g., Obregon, et al.) and the oligarchical traditions of the antihumanist Spanish *Reconquista*, a constitution which is otherwise informally known as the continuing Mexican (humanist) revolution.

During the middle of the nineteenth century, the Mexican humanist tradition was centered around the Kantian Benito Juarez, who gained the leadership of his nation and proceeded toward putting into motion the humanist policies shared by the "French" faction of the eighteenth century Borbon court and by their allies the American revolutionaries. On the pretexts of the British imperial doctrine of "limited sovereignty" and the collection of Mexico's debt service payments to European bankers, London organized a joint British, French, Spanish invasion and occupation of Mexico. The foreign Legion of Napoleon III was assigned the duty of looting the Mexican population in behalf of the London bankers. This forerunner of fascist economic policies was nominally legitimized by the installation of the Hapsburg Maximilian on the Mexican throne. London's adherence to the "Persian model" showed clearly.

London's Mexican project was contingent on the success of London's companion project for dividing the United States itself into several squabbling tyrannies. Rothschild agent August Belmont identified those objectives with shameless candor in his correspondence of that period. A Confederacy, based on chattel slavery and ruled by a slave-owning oligarchy, was to rule in the southeast, under the custody in part of London Rothschild agent and Confederate Treasurer Judah Benjamin. The Western states were to be split away under British influence. (British agents centered in British Columbia treat the states of Washington and Oregon as colonies about to be recovered by Canada to the present day. One cannot understand the politics of a certain senator from Washington unless one understands this point.)

The labor-industrialist alliance rallied around the Clay-Carey Whig--Neoplatonic humanist--Abraham Lincoln, by the end of 1862 proved itself in the process of defeating the British project to destroy the United States. During 1863, the British monarchy dropped the project, and also abandoned the Mexican project to the unfortunate Napoleon III and his puppet Maximilian.

Much is made, too much, of the prominence of names such as Rothschild, Mendelssohn, Oppenheimer, and so forth in London's evil operations against Germany, France, the United States. The role of these Jewish financial houses correlates, a bit too quickly and conclusively in the minds of some, with the role of Jewish financial families in the horrors which have beset civilization during the period since the eighth century BC. A brief summary of the relevant observations should be included at this point, to show the folly of the "international Jewish conspiracy."

Public Domain

Benito Juarez

According to admissions conceded by Winston Churchill at the close of the last world war, there were two points of the Nazi regime at which the British had the option of ridding Germany of the Nazi-pest. The first was during 1938, when Admiral Canaris and members of the military general staff had an operation in place for overthrowing Hitler.   Winston Churchill personally intervened to prevent the plot from being carried through. During the war itself, Allen Dulles and others had established links with generals and others prepared to dump Hitler, the conspiracy which ultimately expressed itself as the "generals' plot."   Churchill once again directly intervened to prevent support of this plot. This Churchill admitted to have been British government policy (omitting mention of his personal role in the matter). Churchill's reply to the parliamentary question, credibly reported to have been drafted by the same Hugh Trevor-Roper who sponsored the postwar doctrine of German "collective guilt," emphasized that Britain did not support the overthrow of Hitler, because His Majesty's government preferred Hitler to his opponents in each instance.

That matter highlights in the sharpest fashion the nature of the relationship between the British monarchy's "court Jews," such as the House of Rothschild, and the forces which actually rule Britain.   The Rothschilds, in particular, have shown themselves persistently, fearfully perceptive of that reality, struggling to secure the added protection of the highest possible aristocratic titles for each branch of their family.   In a sense, the Rothschilds are a nominal and important part of the British aristocracy, but no Jew could ever become truly an insider to the most crudely anti-Semitic stratum of power existing on earth today.

The phenomenon exemplified for popular contemplation by the name Rothschild is, from the Jewish side, the pursuit of the policy of "Jewish survival" on the terms traditionally adopted by a majority of "court Jews" over the centuries--especially since the thirteenth century. Some Jews in that stratum are known to view the matter explicitly in those terms.   On grounds of overwhelming evidence, one assumes that most members of "court Jewish" families either attempt to hide the issue from themselves whenever possible as some are known to do, or view it less blindly in essentially the indicated terms.

It is by being indispensable to their oligarchical Black Guelph masters, accomplishing for those masters what the masters could not accomplish otherwise for themselves, that the "court Jew" survives as a "court Jew." In this fashion, by virtue of this often morally wretched and always degrading sort of outstanding service to his oligarchical masters, the "court Jew" produces evidence apparently supporting the myth of the "the international Jewish conspiracy." What is the origin of the Rothschilds? Out of the ranks of Germany's "court Jews." What is the origin of the Jewish financial houses known as the Oppenheimers, the Mendelssohns? The same. Jewish fear is key.

It is against the background of events so exemplified that one probes the British oligarchical mind to locate the criteria which governed London's decision to sponsor Bismarck as its "man in the Prussian Chancellory." Prince Albert was explicit. The Prussian aristocracy needed to be led into better informed British oligarchical ways of doing things, to understand the importance of the charades of "liberalism" as a means for strengthening--and masking--the autocratic, oligarchical power behind the Charade. The essential thing, excluding all those criticisms

London did moot or may have mooted concerning the Prussian oligarchy, was to promote the "Persian model"--to proceed pragmatically toward the "feudalist" utopia to which Black Guelph tradition remains committed to the present date.

Advance the oligarchical cause *pragmatically*: that is British-centered Black Guelph policy. Abandon a vulnerable flank here. Seek to position the influence of the oligarchy advantageously there. Plant the seeds of future strategic oligarchical advantage where nothing more is feasible. Meanwhile, move constantly to isolate and destroy the Platonic-Neoplatonic influences everywhere, under all conditions, whether as political forces, as national policies, as factional policies, or in the sciences, music, literature, and so forth.

The case of the North American Confederacy is exemplary.[1] By a narrow squeak, chattel slavery was not outlawed with the establishment of the U.S. Constitution. The need for the votes from Virginia was crucial on this connection. However, the United States was committed to ending chattel slavery, until the close of the Napoleonic wars in Europe. Britain's control of the Holy Alliance, of the high seas of commerce and world trade placed the isolated United States in the position, aided by corrupted New England commercial interests, in which an increase in black chattel slavery was imposed upon the United States, an increase accelerated by the election of British agent-of-influence Andrew Jackson to the U.S. Presidency.

The thrust of Jackson's and Van Buren's policies was to wreck the United States' previous policy of scientific and industrially centered technological progress, and to impose a "zero growth," rurally oriented policy. The promotion of black chattel slavery was an integral part of this operational policy.

This policy of promoting black chattel plantation slavery had two distinguishable features. First, economically, the looting of the soil and slaves' bodies and minds in cotton production represented a looting of the internal economy of the United States in favor of London financial interests, with a portion of the theft paid off to both United States financial and commercial interests as well as the plantation oligarchy. Second, this British theft fostered the development of the seeds of the "Persian model" in the United States, the emergence of a plantation-centered oligarchical class of slave owners allied to London-linked monetarist financial interests centered in New Orleans, New York, and Boston. The most conspicuous of those financial interests were U.S. agents of the London Rothschilds.

From Aaron Burr and the Gallatin family, New York-centered British agents and agents of influence controlled the national leadership of the Democratic Party. Van Buren and his puppet Andrew Jackson exemplify this, as do Pierce, Buchanan and 1864 Democratic nominee McClellan. It was the alliance of southern slave-owning oligarchs and monetarist financial and commercial interests which controlled the United States in varying degrees of domination from 1829 through 1860.

Likewise, only by tracing such policies to their roots in the cult of Apollo, to show how the British mentality has been evolved as a species-mentality, can one comprehend the criteria which governed London's choice of Bismarck and Prussia. Without knowing the sweep of history as a process, one can not competently understand any of its parts.

ARCHEOLOGY

Now. we resume the clarification of historiographical categories of method.

In *archeology,* one assembles the shards of available evidence, to the *intermediate* purpose of reconstructing a working-model conception of the society under study.

At this point, one has what might be described as the intermediate model. At this phase, the work of the archeologist suffers flaws analogous to those of the credulous historical narrative form. This phase is indispensable, but does not represent material which of itself is reliable for adducing historiographical knowledge.

To develop the "intermediate model," the work of the archeologist focuses on what was constructed, how it was constructed, and to what use it was employed. By organizing the study of this subject matter in terms of labor time and amounts of household consumption of the population as a whole, archaeological studies can be advanced to a high degree of rigor in accounting for the general features of a culture. In a more useful sort of site or group of sites, the evolution of the culture in these terms provides the most advantageous and a relatively rigorous reconstruction of the sort indicated.

The danger is that the study of the matter is concluded on that level of investigation. To put the matter crudely, but otherwise usefully, the emphasis on the "objective" evidence deprecates the decisive "subjective" side of the culture.

Human practice as a whole is not "objective." Something happens. That might be termed "objective." Yet, one such objective occurrence does not lead directly to a human action in response in an objective way. *Man responds to the stimulating event "subjectively,"* interprets its import and character *"subjectively,"* and selects his response (or, non-response) *"subjectively."* In first approximation, historiography focuses on the "subjective," determining linkage between an "objective" occurrence and responsive "objective" human action. This locates the crucial, "subjective" area of investigation, but does not in itself represent yet competent historiography. The question is how that "subjective" behavior is itself determined, whence and how that manifest way of seeing and responding to the world is developed.

In the absence of literary records, or with aid of only some fragments of literary or protoliterary records, that subjective side of the archaeological record must be interpolated. Unfortunately, most efforts of this sort extant are deceptively plausible, specious, and wrong. The same sort of rigor employed in determining how paleolithic man produced stone tools must be applied to the "technology" of development of ruling sets of ideas. This can not be done on the basis of archeology. We must develop *epistemology* for this work by working backward from history as such, by first applying archaeological methods to the historical period, and thus develop a rigorous method to be applied to the archaeological periods as such.

For one brief example, on the basis of knowing crucial features of the history from the eighth century BC, one can project judgments upon the subjective side of sites from the middle of the third millennium BC, and so forth. How this is to be accomplished, and how we may be certain that such methods are valid, we shall demonstrate in due course in this report. For the present instant, it is sufficient to announce that there can be no competent archaeological historiography without commanding the secrets of the "inner elites."

HUMAN PALEONTOLOGY

It may be noted that we employ "human paleontology" here in an included sense which is more commonly associated with the rubric "anthropology." The compelling reasons for our preference will be qualified in due course below.

Otherwise, the reader should be forewarned that *human paleontology,* properly understood, is the uniquely competent premise for all scientific knowledge, competent historiography included. Consequently, a certain intensity of focus is supplied for that aspect of our report. Not only are we concerned to communicate the secrets of the "inner elite," but also to reformulate them from the standpoint of insights and knowledge not available entirely to our predecessors.

We take up this matter now, beginning by treating the subcategory in question as we treated the other two facets of historiography, and then proceed to the deeper issues.

Human paleontology is occupied in a minor, if not insignificant way, with the varieties of hominids and other matters of physical, or biological anthropology. This feature of the investigation gains importance as our attention focuses inclusively on those characteristic features of the human species' behavior which distinguishes our species from all other anthropoids and hominids, *the power of reason.* This distinction, we are obliged to assume, correlates with some specific biological distinction associated with human processes of mentation, even though the specific biological "substrate" in which that distinction is essentially located may not yet have been defined for investigation. We know that such a distinction exists, and are therefore obliged to pursue the nonbiological side of the investigation in such a way that our work will aid in isolating the biological feature of the matter. If that rigor were not observed, then the entirety of our work would suffer a correlated incompetence.

The proper, principal concern of human paleontology is the study of the development of the human species as a whole, a universality, through study of cultures over long sweeps of time.

Although human paleontology has some incidental overlaps of included techniques with animal paleontology, the evolution of human culture is a feature of the human species' existence which compares only with successful biological differentiation of more advanced varieties and species in animal paleontology. All animals but man are categorically limited, by variety, and species, in their *range* of behavioral possibilities. This works to the effect that this *range* of possible variations in species-reproductive behavior is delimited as if by genetic inheritance. Human culture has, overall, successfully evolved to an effect approximated in the plant and animal kingdoms generally only by the emergence of biologically superior varieties and species. It is that feature of the cultural evolution of mankind which is the essential, primary subject-matter of human paleontology, and which absolutely distinguishes the subject, human paleontology, from the subject of animal paleontology.

There is a correlated difficulty arising from this distinction. Although paleontological evidence dates hominid existence to the Pleistocene according to prevailing estimates, it cannot be assumed that the present human species dates from the onset of that period. Skeletal fragments and a scattering of some artifacts do not enable us to rigorously or conclusively distinguish among hominid "relatives" or "ancestors" who lacked characteristic human qualities of reason and the modern, human species which possesses that distinguishing species-power. The fact that chimpanzees, gorillas, and baboons include the use of "tools" within their range of behaviors in the wild state suggests, usefully, that a certain amount of tool-use may be associated with a species having a human-like skeleton but lacking the power of reason. Until the subsumed issues are resolved, we date human paleontology as an investigation to the Pleistocene, with the provision that adoption of this period has the function of defining the span *within which* we may locate more precisely the emergence of species-man.

The intrinsic methodological defect of "anthropology" as heretofore defined is that its adopted [missing text--editor]tion backwards to this or that notion of a "primeval horde." The fact of the matter is that the power to evolve culture, in the directed way man has secularly advanced his culture since the paleolithic, *is the distinguishing quality the human species,* the quality by which we can distinguish the human species from other, inferior hominids. This distinction separates species-man from the hominids of any hypothesized "primeval horde."

Modern biological research has pointed to some helpful points in this connection. It is now determined that the notion of genetic determination of species and varieties is inherently defective. A heritable varietal change in a species can be induced "environmentally" without genetic variation.[2] The experimental evidence to this effect is conclusive, and already locates the functions of genetic material as heretofore defined within a much larger process which is actually determining. Closer study of the role of the ribosomes shows itself to be a fruitful, if not yet conclusive approach to comprehension of the actually determining processes.[3] What this current line of biological research implies is that without alteration of what is ordinarily considered genetic material, a heritable alteration in the hominid stock could be introduced to the effect of producing a new variety. If this new variety were distinguished by a suitably significant change from other varieties, we should be obliged to consider the new variation a new species on that account.

It is desirable to achieve rigorously defined answers. It is indispensable, first, to have rigorously defined questions. It is such questions which properly

The fact of the matter is that the British colonial system has always followed the instruction of Adam Smith's Wealth of Nations, the policy that populations should be kept wherever possible in a backward state of economic and cultural development relative to Britain itself. This was the feature of Adam Smith against which the American Revolution was fought. It is also a fact that the British colonial office pursued a political doctrine of "cultural relativism" with respect to colonial peoples in general, and promoted that doctrine

as anthropological propaganda, as a part of the effort of the London School of Economics and other institutions to recruit agents for British service and interest from among the natives of the nations they proposed to keep in cultural backwardness.

define science, questions to which we possess only sometimes satisfying answers.

The subject of human paleontology is the empirical investigation of the characteristic of the human species' capability for social evolution from lower into higher forms of knowledge and social practice. This standpoint takes man of this distinction as a species, denying the existence of culture as a development within a precultural "primeval horde." This subject demands its own, appropriate methods of historiography, which we define at some length below.

It is to be granted that the British and their dupes take officially a strong public stand against a principle of cultural evolution, proposing instead the dogma of "cultural relativism."

It would be nonetheless an insult to Oxford and Cambridge to assume that their inner circles actually believe their own publicized propaganda in behalf of "cultural relativism" as an anthropological-scientific thesis. Such propaganda is created for the stultification of the credulous. There is overwhelming evidence that the inner circles of the British intelligentsia are confidently convinced of the very opposite to what they teach credulous fools.

The fact of the matter is that the British colonial system has always followed the instruction of Adam

Smith's *Wealth of Nations,* the policy that populations should be kept wherever possible in a backward state of economic and cultural development relative to Britain itself. This was the feature of Adam Smith against which the American Revolution was fought. It is also a fact that the British colonial office pursued a political doctrine of "cultural relativism" with respect to colonial peoples in general, and promoted that doctrine as anthropological propaganda, as a part of the effort of the London School of Economics and other institutions to recruit agents for British service and interest from among the natives of the nations they proposed to keep in cultural backwardness. This is otherwise an old propaganda trick of the cult of Apollo, the characteristic feature of its cult of Dionysus, as exemplified by the case of al-Ghazali.

The inner circles of the British intelligentsia are not so stupid as to believe their own propaganda on this issue. It cannot be seriously proposed that they do not know that cultural evolution is efficient; *it is certain that they do believe that continued cultural evolution is contrary to the utopian goals of the Black Guelph oligarchy.*

PALEONTOLOGICAL METHODS

Modern historiography properly combines the results and methods appropriate to all three subcategories of historiography into a single methodology. The proper methods for human paleontology are the foundation for the elaboration of historiography--and also the axiomatics of all scientific knowledge--as a whole.

Since human paleontology's essential, primary subject matter is the qualitative difference, *human reason,* between man and the animal species, it is the rigorous focus upon evidence most directly and universally bearing upon that difference which is the proper kernel of all historiography.

The first approximation of the method required is obtained by focusing on the problem of *human ecological population-potential.* This is, at first inspection, the potential number of persons humanity can sustain in a certain mode of producing the necessary means of existence. At second inspection, more accurately, it represents the rate of growth of populations at various levels of population-density in a given mode of production and associated culture. The question is thus posed: *What is the potential rate of expansion of the population which sustains the average individual in a condition of life equal to or better than the condition at a previous, less numerous population? Quality of condition is properly defined in the same way: quality is the equipotentiality of the culture representing individuals in such a condition to maintain at least the same rate of growth of population.*

This admittedly involves a conceptual difficulty for the person of merely an ordinary university or even a more advanced education. The British doctrine of "the inductive sciences," which has become relatively hegemonic in one guise or another. starts with countable objects, and derives notions of ordering and other kinds of relationship through formulations in which the quality of the counted objects is external to the process. Only the quality of the so-called dependent variable is ordinarily assumed to be subject to constructive valuation by formulation. "Self-reflexive functions" are considered outlawed by the dogma of "the

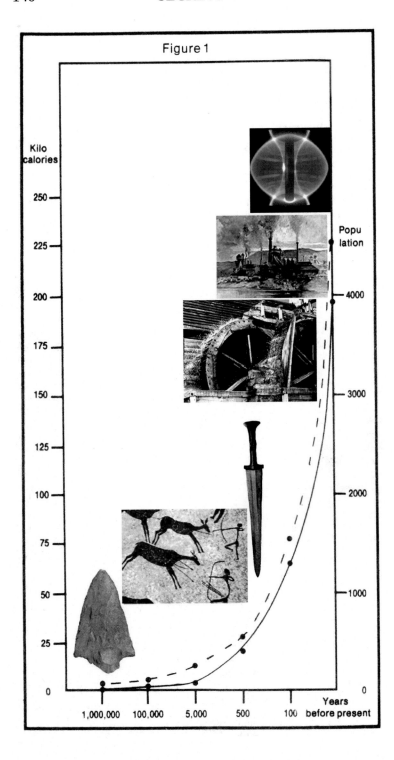

Figure 1

FIGURE 1

The continuing process of scientific invention which defines the human species has produced an exponential increase in the per capita energy consumption of human beings (broken line on graph), demonstrating empirically that the secular increases in human population-potential produced by scientific and cultural progress more than offset the increases in human population (solid line) decried by British-controlled environmentalists and Malthusians.

The time periods shown correspond to fundamental divisions of human history: paleontological history (2-3 million to about 5000 years before present), characterized by stone tools and slowly improving methods of hunting and gathering; archaeological history, beginning around 5000 years ago when a great increase in human per capita energy density was produced with the widespread introduction of solar power in agriculture along with bronze-working techniques; and history as such, the modern period in which the introduction of such technologies as (in the most recent periods) fossil fuels and nuclear energy has rapidly multiplied the energy density available for production.

inductive sciences."[4] Yet, we have admittedly introduced a "self-reflexive function" here. It is the inductive-science dogma which is in error, not our definition given just above.

Beginning with that rough definition of ecological population-potential, we can refine this notion effectively only by considering the conceptual problems which arise as we study the processes through which the mode of production is bettered, and as we at the same time more rigorously define the criteria which determine what is a betterment of the mode of existence.

The first such conceptual difficulty which might pop into view is this. As the mode of culture changes, the requirements of consumption by individuals are altered. Consequently, we cannot compare successive states of cultural development with the included assumption that the normative spectrum of consumption required for the first case is appropriate for the second. Also, we cannot assume that a linear function can account for the transformation

involved. Related conceptual problems will be faced as we proceed.

Changes in ecological population-potential are effected to human advantage through advances in mode of culture, in which advances in mode of production are decisive. These changes originate modally as discoveries mediated through individuals, which become more or less universalized for that culture's practice through, typically, the transmission of such an individual's discovery to numerous others.

This peculiarity of the individual defines the powers of reason (creative discovery) of the individual person as a *singularity* which characterizes the human species as a species. We shall develop the significance of that in due course.

Historically (paleontologically), the cumulative effect of such successful discoveries is a secular trend of increase in the number of calories of useful energy commanded by the average individual engaged in production. This secular increase in per capita energy density of production has in fact risen secularly. Empirically, the cultural progress of the human species correlates with an exponential rate of increase of per capita energy-density for production (cf. *Figure 1*).

Not all cultures have maintained such advance. In general, those strains of cultural progress which are most rapid determine a superior rate of population potential for the branches of culture involved. Stagnating cultures collapse, retrogress, and so forth. In this way the branches of culture which maintain progress determine the largest portion of the human population.

This is not contrary to the fact of population expansion in the developing sector today. The recent tendencies for expansion of those populations are the consequence of European culture. However, because of the City of London's domination of the world financial markets, and because of related malignant influences, the growth of population in developing nations, itself caused by more advanced European cultural influences, appears to represent a problem. This is not a problem because of the numbers of persons existing, or population growth rates.

The two extremes of today's civilization, nuclear reactor and backward peasant and donkey, illustrated in today's Pakistan. "It is man's movement away from labor-intensive forms of production into what are presently capital-intensive forms of increasing emphasis upon 'artificial labor,' which defines the world-line of human survival and progress. Conversely, the shift from capital-intensive, energy-intensive forms of production toward labor-intensive forms of production can have only one consequence: large-scale economic genocide against the populations so murderously oppressed."

Using presently available nuclear-energy technology and imminently available fusion technologies, the world would have already the technology to maintain a population of tens of billions of persons at current European standards. The problem is that the social productivity of populations kept at "labor-intensive" levels at or near barbarism is inadequate to sustain those persons.

There is a recurring "resources problem," of course; however, this problem has no resemblance to the hoaxes circulated under that rubric by Ralph Nader, the Club of Rome, or Barry Commoner.

From early in the existence of the human species, man has been perpetually, or with frequent recurrence, confronted at each such point with what a contemporary "Club of Rome" could have argued to be an "insuperable limit to growth" with as much finality as the actual Club of Rome argues presently. This problem existed when the human population of the earth could be counted in mere millions, and repeatedly so thereafter. Yet, in all those branches of cultural evolution which have led into modern civilization, man has repeatedly overcome what "environmentalist" maniacs of those times might have decreed to be "insuperable limits to growth."

The British oligarchy's inner circle of intelligentsia knows this to be a fact. Privately, as some examples attest in fact, they should consider themselves insulted (privately) in respect of their intelligence if one accused them of actually believing the rubbish published by the Club of Rome. Similarly, since the British have developed and operated nuclear energy plants, the British elite knows that nuclear energy production by established standards is the safest sort of energy production yet in existence.

They know, and will sometimes concede privately, that the Club of Rome thesis and "environmentalism" generally are hoaxes, fit only for the consumption of very foolish, very credulous dupes. After all, it was they who ordered that those hoaxes be concocted.

As in the instance of "cultural revolution," *their point is that they do not wish to maintain technological progress; they are only wicked, not stupid; they are not such abysmal idiots that they do not believe technological progress could not solve all the present ecological problems.* It was to aid them in mobilizing adequate political support from masses of fools, to block  technological progress, that they promoted the Club of Rome's hoax. They generated a myth to persuade the hysterical donkeys of plebeia that technological progress was undesirable--because they are determined to bring on the "new dark age" out of which they aim to establish enduring rule for their "feudalist" utopia.

At first glance, the pseudo-limits to growth have been successively overcome by our species through increased per capita energy for production. The use of tools, the development of the simplest forms of agriculture, the simplest forms of livestock raising, increase the usable energy commanded by a calorie of human biological effort. The application of fire and its cultural derivatives have the same effect. The "reducing power" of the species relative to existing forms of man-altered nature is increased. The increase in calories of "artificial labor" commanded by a calorie of human biological effort tends toward a qualitative decline in costs of "primary materials" per calorie of human biological effort, such that marginal or out-of-reach primary resources of a lower state of culture become the abundant, cheap resources of a new stage of progress of culture.

It is man's movement away from labor-intensive forms of production into what are presently capital intensive forms of increasing emphasis upon "artificial labor," which define the world-line of human survival and progress. Conversely, the shift from capital intensive forms of production can have only one consequence: large-scale genocide against the populations so murderously oppressed.

The British who propose labor-intensive methods know this. They propose labor-intensive "full employment" methods precisely because they intend to reduce the earth's population to the order of between one and two billion persons by the end of the century. They create movements for labor-intensive full employment measures, such as the U.S. draft Humphrey Hawkins legislation, because they wish to induce populations to willfully mass-murder themselves in this emulation of the lemming.

Increased energy-density is indispensable for maintaining as well as advancing human culture. Yet, it is not undifferentiated scalar increases in energy per capita which enable man to survive. It is inventions. It is inventions which make possible increases in the energy-density of production. It is inventions which make possible the effective conversion of that augmented energy-density into useful forms of production.

The effort to reconcile two interconnected causes, *energy* and *reason*, into something equivalent to a single "equation" points us immediately in the direction of the most fundamental issues of scientific knowledge. Energy is ordinarily measured in calories, watts, and so forth. These are all *scalar* measures. In what units is human reason to be measured? The concern of Thales and other Ionians for the combined action of *mind, fire* (energy), and *continuous primary substance* cannot seem so unimportant a conception as Aristotle and his admirers have purported to make the issue--it is indeed so fundamental that the import of Thales' work is to this day concealed with aid of British. frauds.

We shall turn attention to the subsumed physics of that problem subsequently. It is indispensable to note the existence of such a problem at this state of the report, so that it can be temporarily set to one side, and that we may proceed to examine one crucial facet of this matter seemingly independently of the physics problem as such. We shall show, subsequently, why *energy cannot be fundamentally a scalar magnitude,* and under what circumstances it might nonetheless appear to be a scalar.

THE MEANING OF SCIENCE

So far, we have outlined the premises for the following judgments concerning historiography. History, in both its narrowest and broadest meanings, is the history of the human species. Consequently, it is the history of the distinguishing characteristics of the human species, the history of reason, and of the consequences of actions taken according to or contrary to reason by individuals and societies. The advances in ecological population-potential, which determine whether or not the species shall continue to exist, determine successive advances (secularly, for the species as a whole) in successive forms of culture.

Reason is not applied *ex novo* to raw, precultural conditions, but is always reason informed by an existing culture acting to change (advance) that culture. Hence, history and the internal history of science are inseparable facets of the same inquiry. It is the ordering of the evolution of human culture according to the principles internal to scientific progress which is the primary feature of competent historiography, the standard of reference with whose governance we comprehend inclusively the failures of human history.

Conversely, history so studied is the unique premise for competent scientific knowledge.

The key to scientific method, and thus to the mastery of both science and history, is the method of the Platonic dialogue. This is also properly termed the *dialectical method,* as such a method is associated with Thales, Heraclitus and Plato. It is not, however, the "dialectical method" represented in most of the available literary productions of the Moscow Institute of Marxism-Leninism--even though the kernel of Karl Marx's method was a distillate from the Ionian dialectical method.

This Platonic method has two inseparable facets. As a consequence of its findings, the Platonic method early correctly classified all forms of human knowledge into three primary categories, showing, as we have noted earlier, how the method of the Platonic dialogue ordered the progress of the mental development of the individual from the lowest to the highest of these three levels.

The lowest level is the level of *simple belief,* the level of individual judgment defectively based on narrow experience and informed chiefly by prejudices and mythologies. That is the level of "common sense." or "horse sense." the donkey-like state of the human intellect. The second level is the level of the *understanding,* as defined by Immanuel Kant, for example. It is on this level that underdeveloped and miseducated persons mislocate their definitions of "scientific knowledge." Those misdefinitions of scientific knowledge are what we must expose as fraudulent here. The third, highest level is the level Plato associated with Socratic reason, or, for our purposes here, simply *reason,* the *Vernunft* of whose existence Kant was certain, but whose efficiency he pronounced incomprehensible to the understanding. It is at this level that science properly defined is found.

That is the understanding, and application of science we must outline here.

The Platonic dialogue's method, the dialectical method. is essentially as follows.

It begins with the certainty that all knowledge presumably believed by the individual on the basis of his culture and narrow sense-experience is inherently false because of that very narrowness of its empirical basis. In the way this was defined by Spinoza, such knowledge is *inadequate* or *fictitious*. In the Platonic dialogue, the individual examines his own consciousness in terms of the way this consciousness is consciously mirrored in the thinking of another person(s). The point of this is not to compare different views. If one attributes such a trivial significance to the Platonic dialogue, one condemns oneself to benighted ignorance forever. The object of "mirroring" is to make one's own consciousness an object for, a subject of one's willful consciousness, to make consciousness an object of willful consciousness for itself.

The subject of such willful consciousness of one's own mirrored consciousness is not primarily the "what?" of the consciousness brought under willful scrutiny. The primary subject matter is the "how?" and "why?" of that consciousness. My concern is not simply to discover on what points I may have believed in error; my concern is to discover in my consciousness *how* previously prevailing criteria have led me into error, and *why* I have thought foolishly. The subject of willful consciousness of consciousness is willful mastery of the *method* of conscious thought. The object of the Platonic method is to develop in oneself an effective method of thinking, of judgment, to reduce consciousness itself to a subject of scientific inquiry concerning method.

The first goal of the Platonic method is *negation,* is to break out of the narrowness of fictitious, false knowledge ("common sense," "practical experience"). I must, in first approximation, determine what methods of conscious judgment will actually solve problems without significant error over entire ranges of experience.

These method-specific ranges of experience are termed *categories* of knowledge. In turn, what is termed a *category* is determined by the differences in specific methods of judgment required for various aspects of knowledge (understanding). Another term for category is a relative *universality*. For example, physics, chemistry, botany, internal medicine, economics, and so forth have been subcategories of knowledge on these grounds, even though they may otherwise overlap.

To arrive at methods of thought by which one has mastered such a universality of knowledge methodologically from the standpoint of relatively best contemporary levels of practice, is to have arrived at a condition of *understanding* for that category. However, this does not remove the case in which a person has an understanding of physics and yet is a donkey in matters of, for example. internal medicine and economics. To characterize persons as persons of *understanding in general* has a special meaning. It means that the philosophical outlook of the person toward categories of knowledge which he has not yet mastered in particular is methodologically in correspondence with the principles of understanding--although he may not yet have achieved the competence of particular understanding in that category. It means that his philosophical outlook, his governing sense of personal social identity is governed by the methodological principles of understanding.

Consequently, derived from or subsumed under this level of mental development, we have given to us the usual misdefinition of scientific knowledge among educated persons. In the case of the mathematical sciences, science is usually associated with the range of conceptual apparatus currently developed by the culture in the indicated categories. There is another, worse meaning, we merely identify at this instant, the meaning given to "science" by the dogma of "the inductive sciences."

In *reason,* we advance a qualitative step beyond the mere understanding. In understanding, we seek to extend present elementary knowledge and special methods "horizontally," so to speak, to fill out the extent of knowledge in each category, to establish coherent connections among categories, and to correct included errors in the body of existing knowledge in an ordinary fashion. Although creative-mental activity is essential to this work, it is largely unconscious mental activity, and so appears only as a tool of the effort; it is generally regarded as something outside the domain to which it is applied transiently in acts of creativity. In progressing from mere understanding to reason, we apply the same Platonic method to the inadequacies of understanding that was applied, to achieve understanding, to donkey-like states of "common sense."

There is nothing properly mystical in this, no mumbo jumbo, yoga-like meditative gimmickry, or any "black magic" of that sort. Geniuses are grown, cultivated, not produced miraculously out of donkeys sucking on some fortuitously acquired philosopher's stone.

The inadequacy of existing scientific knowledge generally is that it must be superseded, to arrive at a higher level of scientific knowledge. This is not solved by the effort to leap abruptly into the next qualitative development of scientific knowledge.

The *process* of progressive evolution of scientific knowledge must be made itself an object for willful consciousness. It is the internal history of progress of scientific and related knowledge. approached in this way, which enables consciousness to willfully abstract the element of progress from the consciousness of scientific knowledge in particular. In other words, the subject of consciousness is transformed from the conscious contemplation of an existing body of scientific knowledge, into comprehension of the process which characterizes the historical progress of scientific knowledge. It is this element of science, the *motion of scientific progress*, from which we abstract for consciousness the *method* for willfully effecting scientific progress. The mastery of that indicated method, developed for knowledge in that way, is *reason*.

In that way, the kinds of unconscious process of thought by which the creative person otherwise on the level of mere understanding produces the exceptional insights turning up seemingly so abruptly in his conscious understanding, are brought into willful consciousness by the Platonic method, and thus made the ruling criteria of what then becomes ordinary, willful consciousness of reason for that person.

The way in which the contemporary nonsense-version of the "dialectical method" came into circulation, e.g. the case of the Moscow Institute, was that certain persons encumbered with the duty of professing that method, and yet without the slightest acquaintance with it, applied, at best, the mere understanding to the task of composing glosses on what seemed appropriate passages from Hegel, Marx, Engels and so forth, often with reference to Lenin's *Materialism and Empirio-Criticism* and "Philosophical Notebooks" added.

This method--in its actuality--is not only a method for developing geniuses, or, more modestly and realistically, for developing people's mental powers in directions converging upon genius. It is the indispensable point of reference for competently defining the lawful ordering of the universe. We shall turn to develop that facet of the point now, and return, later, to complete the notion of science on the basis of such grounding development.

THE PROOF OF SCIENCE

The proof of scientific knowledge is essentially that through the improved social practice with which its application is associated, man advances the power of his society in terms of ecological population-potential. Although the individual invention is expressed in this, the individual invention, defined only as an individual invention, does not define such a proof of the knowledge embodied in itself. It is the generality, or relative universality of invention, a generality which is at least implicitly expressible as a quality of prevailing scientific practice, which a society tests, tests by the success of its existence through progress.

In a limited sense, therefore, the efficacy of existing scientific knowledge, as demonstrated in the indicated way, does prove that the laws attributable to scientific knowledge are in *some form of* correlation with the lawful ordering of the universe. However, the paradoxes of existing scientific knowledge, in particular, conclusively indicate that the existing body of scientific knowledge is not competently representative of comprehensive knowledge of universal laws, indeed that the flaws of existing mathematical~scientific knowledge are axiomatic on this account.

This apparently insuperable problem begins to evaporate once we shift the focus from an existing body of scientific knowledge to the history of progress of human scientific and related knowledge. At no point has the prevailing body of knowledge according to understanding been adequately in correspondence with reality. Yet, in respect of all those advances in understanding which are rankable as advances by the criterion of ecological population-potential, the progress in understanding determining such advances is progress in correspondence with the lawful ordering of the universe.

In other words, no form of *understanding*, mathematical physics as presently defined included, could possibly be in actual correspondence with the lawful ordering of the universe, but *reason* is. One could avoid the point, out of fear no doubt, and say merely that the successive, qualitative advances in physics appear to converge, as if asymptotically, upon some "true physics" which is in correspondence with fundamental laws. That view would be more credible to the taste of prevailing mythologies, but is false for that very reason. It is also a useless compromise, since such a fearful, conservative observation contributes nothing which points our attention in direction of fruitful scientific progress.

The problem which such fearful evasions of the point most explicitly incur is that the level of understanding, exemplified by mathematical physics, involves axiomatic assumptions like those associated with mathematics as such. Once we shift our focus away from the standpoint of mere scientific knowledge to the process of historical progress of scientific knowledge, such axiomatic difficulties begin to vanish.

The formal solution to this problem for mathematical physics began to emerge for direct, conscious comprehension through the combined efforts of Riemann and Cantor. We sum up here the point to be extracted from those sources.

Throw away the mistaken notion of a universe which can be represented by the heurisms of a fixed, n-dimensional geometry. Imagine instead, a universe whose characteristic, defining feature as a whole is a constant self-elaboration from the equivalent of any given n-geometry into an (n+ l)-geometry. Now, rather than considering the symbols of "n," "n+1," "n+2," as counting the numbers of geometric-like dimensions of such a universe, let "n," "n+1," "n+2," and so forth denote different qualities of universe, in the sense of *transfinites* as developed by Cantor.

Now, to illustrate the implications of this, we note the following applicable case, without, we trust, implying that this illustration offered is exclusive.

We have at hand a case which corresponds to such an "n+1," "n+2" ordering. If the world of prevailing physics and chemistry knowledge is taken as such, this can be termed the "n-dimensional" continuum. Mathematically interpreted in presently prevailing ways, that continuum is presumed to be characterized by entropy. It is not entropic in fact, but the prevailing analysis of such an "n-dimensional" continuum might be and is usually construed to suggest that, on condition such a continuum were the universe. The phenomena of living processes correspond then to an "n+1" continuum, which is characteristically negentropic. The phenomena of creative reason in living beings, human cultural evolution, represents an "n+2" continuum, which is of a higher order of negentropy than the "n+1."

Moreover, "n+2" is efficient with respect to both "n" and "n+1," and "n+1" is efficient with respect to "n." Furthermore, "n+1" "historically" developed out of "n," and "n+2" "historically" out of "n+1."

That is, incidentally, the basis in conception on which Riemann explicitly developed all his principal contributions, and is also the basis on which Cantor, with explicit reference to relevant aspects of the work of Leibniz and Nicholas of Cusa, developed his complementary notion of transfinites.

The conception of reason employed by Riemann and Cantor was not original to them. This conception of the fundamental ordering of the universe was first documented, to our present knowledge, by Ibn Sina, in his *Metaphysics*--as the conception of the "necessary existent," and also by Cusa, as his conception of the "Non-Other." This is also the guiding conception of Gottfried Leibniz, the "secret" of his *Monadology,* and of his development of the notion of "inertia" with aid of a methodological criticism of Descartes derived directly from this order of conception of universal law.

Two principal observations have to be made immediately on the points just developed. First, a matter of some importance, "n," "n+1," and "n+2" correspond significantly to the three qualities of the human intellect in the Platonic method. This not merely because they represent three levels, but because the characteristics of mental life at each level correspond to the epistemology of experience as seen from each of these levels. Second, the characteristics of neither an "n," "n+1" nor "n+2" continuum can correspond to the real universe. Only the principle which characterizes the going over from an "n" to "n +1" to "n +2," and so forth, can be the higher, relative transfinite in correspondence with the actual lawful ordering of the universe. (cf. *Figure 2*)

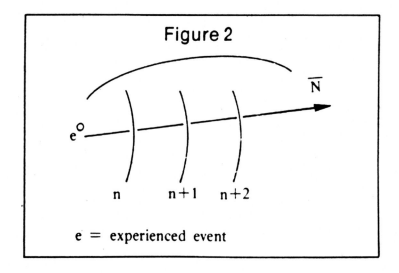

Figure 2

e = experienced event

Again, the only aspect of human consciousness which is in correspondence with such a transfinite--or *transinvariant*--principle of the universe, is the quality of progress in human scientific knowledge, rather than any specific, subsumed scientific knowledge as such. The adducing of that principle, in turn, provides the methodological principle for ordering thought to the effect of willfully "energizing" the progress of scientific knowledge. That is the method of rigorous hypothesis. That is the meaning of the dialectical method, the method of rigorously developing valid hypotheses.

The method employed is the Platonic method of *negation*, as applied from the standpoint of the level of reason. The method of negation means to isolate those axiomatic fallacies of existing knowledge (understanding) which bear upon crucial-experimental problems confronting us. The qualitative elimination of the axiomatic fallacy permits the defining of experiments which can be represented in terms of quantitative relationships. The essential, underlying test of the validity of an hypothesis (as an hypothesis) posed in this way, is the test of whether the hypothesis, if successfully demonstrated, implies a means for increasing the negentropy of human practice.

Such hypotheses are defined by Riemann as "unique hypotheses." Their distinction in effect is that they test the laws of the universe for a category of knowledge, rather than merely testing the applicability of extension of established principles to a problem without involving a testing of general laws. Such hypotheses are more commonly, less rigorously, termed "crucial experimental hypotheses."

In the case such an hypothesis fails experimentally, no loss. The failure of the hypothesis narrows qualitatively our approach to the axiomatic fallacy it attacked, and thus acts as positive progress in knowledge for attacking that axiomatic fallacy in a more effective way.

THE ARISTOTELIAN SUCCESSION

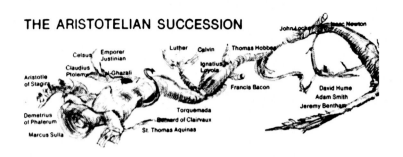

The legacy of Aristotle and his masters in the cult of Delphian Apollo is a succession of criminals, poisoners, practitioners of black magic, plagiarizers and frauds which has maintained an unbroken continuity for more than 2000 years. Operating under a variety of guises, the better to manipulate the gullible, the members of the Aristotelian conspiracy are distinguished by their opposition to technological progress and their fear of the power of human reason. Today's Aristotelians are centered around the Black Guelph Anglo-Dutch oligarchy.

[Names in chart roughly from left to right:]

Marcus Sulla

Demetrius of Pharlerum

Aristotle of Stagira

Claudius Ptolemy

Celsus

Emperor Justinian

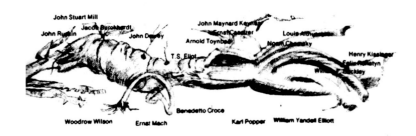

al-Ghazali

St. Thomas Aquinas

Bernard of Clairvaux

Torquemada

Luther

Calvin

Ignatius Loyola

Francis Bacon

Thomas Hobbes

John Locke

Isaac Newton

Jeremy Bentham

Adam Smith

David Hume

John Ruskin

John Stuart Mill

Jacob Burkhardt

Woodrow Wilson

John Dewey

Ernst Mach

T. S. Eliot

Benedetto Croce

Arnold Toynbee

John Maynard Keynes

Ernst Cassirer

Karl Popper

William Yandell Elliot

Noam Chomsky

Louis Althusser

William F. Buckley

Felix Rohatyn

Henry Kissinger

THE CASES OF ARISTOTLE AND NEWTON

On the basis of surviving writings of Plato and of fragments of the work of his predecessors of the Ionian current, it is shown beyond admissible ambiguity that those Ionians and their collaborators were attacking precisely the problems we have so far defined, and also attacking them in a most rigorous and fruitful fashion.

It is clear from the writings attributed to Aristotle, that he not only had direct access to numbers of these Ionian works--some of which he cites--but that he set out deliberately to obfuscate those writings, not only by falsifying his commentaries in a sweeping fashion, but by focusing his frauds upon the most crucial features of such writings. That most crucial feature was, in broadest terms, the Platonic--or dialectical--method, and, emphatically, the method of rigorous scientific hypothesis derived from it.

The same method was employed, with no advance in sophistication of mental exertions, by Francis Bacon and later, by the associates of John Locke in developing the program of the British Royal Society.

Notable is the comparison between Francis Bacon and William Gilbert. Gilbert, a Neoplatonic, competes with Avicennean Roger Bacon as the greatest scientific thinker England ever produced. Francis Bacon, by contrast, was a bungling, unproductive incompetent. It was Gilbert whose *De Magnete* provided Kepler with the indispensable final link for solving the problem of the solar orbits. Both were in the networks linked to Giordano Bruno, linked to the great center of Padua, the accomplishments of the Florentine Academy, and to the rigorous formulation of the method of crucial scientific hypothesis by Nicholas of Cusa. Bacon's obsessive attacks on Gilbert are a degraded scandal, and Bacon's *Novum Organum* a malignant "neo-Aristotelian" hoax.

The point is made clearer by comparing Bacon's attacks on Gilbert with his attacks on the English composer John Bull.[6]

Contrary to the mythology taught by the confused to the credulous in the music departments of our universities, Johann Sebastian Bach did not develop the well-tempered system as such. That system was fully developed by the tenth century Ismaili al-Farabi, whose writings introduced the system to medieval Europe through such influences as Guido Aretino, centuries before Bach. Al-Farabi, writing in the tenth century, reports the well-tempered system to have been very ancient by his own time, and the surviving writings of a contemporary and adversary of Aristotle's corroborate this. Bach's accomplishment was not to develop the well-tempered system. Bach, previously thoroughly schooled in the well-tempered system, accomplished something quite different. Bach resolved the contributions of European vocal polyphony into a lawful, contrapuntal system of musical composition, to the effect that every note of a composition has a well defined lawful significance, including those which represent dissonances.

Later, Beethoven, himself intensely schooled in Bach during childhood, carried Bach's accomplishment a major, qualitative step forward, beyond Bach's formal system of reference, into the principle of self-developing systems of counterpoint as exemplified by Beethoven's own late major works.

Bach's work on methods of composition was not original to him. Exemplary, John Bull taught the well tempered system to bodies of students as a method of composition. Together with his contemporary Sweelinck, Bull was one of the leading masters of the well-tempered system of composition in his time, and part of the heritage directly transmitted to Bach's own teachers.

Bacon drove Bull out of England and caused Bull's writings on music to be destroyed.

Bacon's book-burning orgy is no isolated matter. The British intelligence services hounded Bach into isolation and attempted to suppress all knowledge of his work throughout Europe, to the point that even Bach's virtuoso son was intimidated against performing his father's compositions. A similar operation was deployed against the influence of Beethoven--through Mendelssohn, Richard Wagner, and others.[7] Although the factional issue so expressed was much older, there is a direct, unbroken factional tradition concerning music by the Black Guelph faction from Bacon to the present day. The British-promoted "rock" and the Frankfurt School's promotion of the school of Schoenberg, Webern, et al., are consistent continuations of that issue.

The British neo-Aristotelian music-doctrine was early associated--into the nineteenth century--with the irrationalist doctrine that musical thematic material was properly only an arbitrary selection of tunes, which were agreeable for one or another reason peculiar to the composer, or to the relationship among the composer, performer and audiences. Harmony for the British was merely a matter of an agreeable form of embellishment of

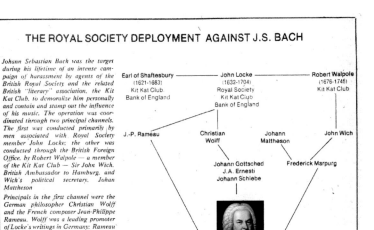

THE ROYAL SOCIETY DEPLOYMENT AGAINST J.S. BACH

Johann Sebastian Bach was the target during his lifetime of an intense campaign of harassment by agents of the British Royal Society and the related British "literary" association, the Kit Kat Club, to demoralize him personally and contain and stamp out the influence of his music. The operation was coordinated through two principal channels. The first was conducted primarily by men associated with Royal Society member John Locke; the other was conducted through the British Foreign Office, by Robert Walpole — a member of the Kit Kat Club — Sir John Wich, British Ambassador to Hamburg, and Wich's political secretary, Johan Mattheson

Principals in the first channel were the German philosopher Christian Wolff and the French composer Jean-Philippe Rameau. Wolff was a leading promoter of Locke's writings in Germany; Rameau mounted a direct polemic against Bach's development of scientific counterpoint, the method of block chord harmonies which is the basis of today's "rock."

Johann Sebastian Bach was the target during his lifetime of an intense campaign of harassment by agents of the British Royal Society and the related British "literary"association, the Kit Kat Club, to demoralize him personally and contain and stamp out the influence of his music. The operation was coordinated through two principal channels. The first was conducted primarily by men associated with Royal Society member John Locke; the other was conducted through the British Foreign Office, by Robert Walpole--a member of the Kit Kat Club--Sir John Wich, British Ambassador to Hamburg, and Wich's political secretary, Johan Mattheson.

Principals in the first channel were the German philosopher Christian Wolff and the French composer Jean-Philippe Rameau. Wolff was a leading promoter of Locke's writings in Germany; Rameau mounted a direct polemic against Bach's development of

*scientific counterpoint, the method of block
chord harmonies which is the basis of today's
"rock."*

the performance of the arbitrary tune; the other forms of
embellishment of the melodic line, for which rococo
performances are notorious, were argued to be a matter of
idiosyncratic taste by the performer. The promotion of,
first, Schoenberg's school, and later "rock" by the British
intelligence services, has the special significance of
introducing the principles of the Phrygian cult of Dionysus
into the neo-Aristotelian doctrine's general application.

From the ancient times, the well-tempered system
was intrinsically associated with an opposite view of both
musical composition and the function of music.

The prevailing mythology of the present-day music
department bears on this issue directly. According to the
neo-Aristotelian doctrine, the musical doctrine of
Pythagoras defines a system of "natural" intervals. On this
premise, with the aid of reference to the mechanics of
vibrating strings, the ignorant edify the dupe with the
doctrine that the Pythagorean scale is a "natural scale," and
that, *therefore,* the well-tempered system is an "artificial
system" adopted for this or that plausible reason. Al-
Farabi's argument shows correctly that this view is nothing
but absurd. The human requirement of the fifth, the
derivation of the octave from this approach, and the fact of
modulation from one mode (or, key) or other within a
composition, illustrates the point that human beings are not

"vibrating strings," and that human music has nothing to do with the purported amusement of inorganic substances.

Music is a sensuous medium of mental creative activity, in which the composer lawfully arrives at relative dissonances in various ingenious ways, within terms of the lawful order of an initial mode. These relative dissonances are resolved as transitions to another lawful mode, . . . and, so on and so forth, such that the resolution of such developed relative dissonances in a composition defines a coherent totality, subsuming several modes and their made-necessary transitional connections. Thus, a good such musical composition resolves this process in the enunciation of a summarizing *stretto* or the equivalent, which, at the completion of the composition, resounds in the hearer's mind as an affirmation that the development which has occurred within the composition is now demonstrated to be lawful in its own right. In other choice of terms, a successful musical composition is a demonstration of the coherence of *freedom* (creative expansion of what is lawful) with *necessity* (that everything must satisfy some form of lawful ordering).

In consequence, music which satisfies the principles of the well-tempered system of composition (and its evolutionary derivatives) is both an abstract form of and also a sensuous exercise of the creative potentialities of the minds of composer, performers, and audiences.

The greatest possibilities for such musical development originate as polyphony ordered in a well tempered system. Thus, where the confused, miseducated dupe says "harmony," the musician says "voices." Each voice, elaborating its material according to the lawful ordering, is in active, lawful relationship to the concurrent voices, also proceeding lawfully. By shifts in accents and intonations, cross-voice "voices" are created, including relative dissonances. In this ordering, there are no "chords" being struck (or strummed) "in harmony" with a vocal melodic line. Every note is the ongoing activity of a voice, every note an activity of a voice which is in polyphonic (contrapuntal) relationship to everything else in the composition. Every voice, every note of each voice, must have a necessary role for the development of the composition, or it should not be sounded.

The folly taught as musical theory in most schools today is most directly derived from the nonsense produced by Rameau, the doctrine of harmony as arbitrary, neo-Aristotelian rules (fixed categories) enslaved to the irrationalist selection of a melodic element. It was this doctrine of Rameau's which the British intelligence services promoted against Bach during the early eighteenth century, and which nonsense has left its embedded influence in the axiomatics of nineteenth century musicological theoretics and their various twentieth century derivatives.

Notable is the nineteenth century "romantic" school, which in its most banalizing aspects substitutes an unhinged and arbitrary obsession with sheer chromaticism as what was deemed an adequate alternative to the rigorously defined dissonance of the contrapuntal development processes of composition.

In consequence of the destructive influence of British intelligence services on music, we have reached the circumstance today at which good musical performers (and a vestige of-a sane musical audience) exist almost entirely because of the influence of Bach, the late Mozart, and Beethoven upon their childhood instrumental (and) other training. In this way they have arrived at an "instinctive" insight into music. Yet, because the musical theory taught is the wretched myths and nonsense of the British influence's effects, virtually no good performer is able to articulate his or her valid insights in the form of musical-theoretical statements--and there are no significant composers. There are those who possess valid "insight" into great music, but virtually none sufficiently familiar with the laws of music to be able to create a musical composition even by standards prevailing during the early nineteenth century, or the modern proper equivalent of such standards.

This indicated attempt to destroy music by Bacon and others was not original to the British neo-Aristotelians, or even their earlier, medieval predecessors. Aristotle himself was the ostensible author of the British neo-Aristotelian doctrine.

In the matter of music as in scientific knowledge generally, Aristotle and his imitators of the British Royal Society followed the same policy, and the same motive. Aristotle's objective, as in his fraudulent commentaries on Plato's and other writings, was to eliminate all evidence of and credit for scientific method, for the method of reason. Just as the principles of musical composition can be formally described only from the Riemannian standpoint we have identified earlier here, so the conceptions of Riemann are nothing but a derivative of the principles of reason in the Platonic-Neoplatonic sense of reason.

The same principle was applied by the British to Germany of the late nineteenth century. Most visibly, from approximately the time of Bismarck's accession to the Prussian Chancellory, but beginning, more modestly, earlier. British influence in Germany focused on promoting two philosophical methods. The first was the so-called neo-Kantian fad; the second was the convergent phenomenology and existentialism leading into the existentialism of the Nazi Martin Heidegger, and more immediately agreeable to post-Bentham varieties of British "philosophical radicalism." The nominal targets of this campaign were G.W.F. Hegel, and actually Immanual Kant himself--the neo-Kantians were in fact predominantly anti-Kantians.

Insofar as Kant defined the problem of *Vernunft* (pure reason), the British hated him. The premises on which Kant argued that the "thing-in-itself" must be incomprehensible to the mere understanding, the British hostilely rejected. They used Kant because he was a famous (and, conveniently, dead) German philosopher, and because the byproducts of his critiques could be perverted to the form of the British doctrine.

The point is crucial; we summarize it here.

The basis of Kant's notion of the incomprehensible "thing in itself" was this.

Kant proceeded from the Platonic definition of the three categories--simple belief, understanding and reason. He also defined the progress from simple belief to understanding in the mode of the Platonic dialectic. The point to be considered is made most succinctly in the second portion of his *Critique Of Practical Reason,* "The Dialectic of Practical Reason." He recognized the existence of reason in the Platonic sense, adding the stipulation that reason must be efficient for practice, that knowledge created by reason was the basis for efficient practice in the world otherwise known to the understanding.

He stumbled at the problem of *pure practical reason* in the following way. Reason, standing "above" the deterministic ordering of the mere understanding, must affect the world in a way (*freedom*) not in conformity with the fixed deterministic rules of the understanding. However--and here is the crux of Kant's problem--since human knowledge of the determination of categories of knowledge is limited to the forms of the understanding, the efficient consequences of reason are unknowable, indeterminate, for the understanding. Hence, the real world, which must embody the efficiency of practical reason, must define existence (the thing-in-itself) in a way which is not comprehensible to the understanding; hence, the thing-in-itself is incomprehensible.

The neo-Kantians (at least, in the main) ignored Kant's argument, and substituted the principle of irrationalist indeterminacy within the nominal form of Kant's formulation of the problem. Instead of Kant's judgment that the efficiency of reason was beyond human comprehension, the neo-Kantians proposed that the thing-in-itself was indeterminate because it was, intrinsically, arbitrarily anarchic. Thus, Thomas Hobbes and John Locke were smuggled into the neo-Kantian's commentaries on Kant.

This was the same result offered by Aristotle. On the one side, Aristotle adopted the appearance of a pure determinist. He proposed fixed, lawful orderings of categories, and so forth. However, embedded within that schema, the elementarity of the irrational takes the place of the problem of the comprehension of the specific lawfulness of reason. So, the Phrygian cult of Dionysus was embedded within the cult of Apollo. Roman stoicism was developed to the same effect by the cult of Apollo as the secularized version of the Apollonian mysticism.

Phenomenology and existentialism are simply such neo-Kantianism or Aristotelianism viewed through the microscope.

The complementary expression of this in contemporary Maoist cults is the secularized theological doctrine of "God is dead." The doctrine's source-rationale is as follows. If God created the universe with fixed universal laws, then by so doing, God precluded his own subsequent willful intervention into the universe. Hence, God may be omniscient, but is certainly impotent. Hence, to take the point a step further, God, because entirely impotent with respect to the universe, is dead with respect to the universe. Furthermore, although the individual will is entirely irrational (arbitrarily anarchistic), the laws of the universe are so fashioned that they succeed despite the anarchy of individuals. The contemporary Maoist doctrine follows: *do whatever you please, what is going to occur will occur anyway.*

On this ground Maoists are secularized strict Lutherans. "The ordering of the world is governed by principles beyond your power to comprehend or change.

What is of concern to you is merely your private exercise of your anarchistic impulses." This is also the doctrine of Bernard of Clairvaux. "You are only efficiently concerned with such matters, the matters of your personal, Hobbesian sub-universe. The fundamental error would be to follow Abelard, to attempt to be the helper of God in the ongoing work of creation. Abelardian elites, such elitists, are the only problem with which you have to deal."

The British purpose behind the neo-Kantian campaign in Germany was the destruction of science. The case of Georg Cantor is exemplary, as is, in a different form, the campaign of Ernst Match and his allies against Max Planck, and the Copenhagen-centered assault on the leading scientific thinkers of the 1920s.

Cantor, the student of Weierstrass, inherited-- Weierstrass's conflict with the wretched, but influential, British-favored Kronecker. Cantor, sensible of the importance of his discoveries, was perplexed by the way--*it seemed to him*--that Kronecker was orchestrating a Europe-wide, successful effort to slander and isolate him. All Europe generally, was turned into what was effectively a "controlled environment," such that even Cantor's supposed friends induced him to capitulate to Kronecker. Cantor broke under this orchestrated pressure, capitulated to Kronecker, and, as a result of this capitulation, went insane. A British operation.

From the foundation of the British Royal Society, its principal dedication was to the destruction of what it termed "continental science." This began--in that form-- with Locke's coordination of attacks against Descartes (echoing Bacon's campaign against Bull and Gilbert),

continued with Leibniz--next regarded the chief danger--
and continued through the nineteenth century. During the
nineteenth century, Faraday was obsessed by this impulse.
Maxwell was governed by it.[8] Pasteur was hated, harassed
by British influences in France. Riemann's reputation as
well as Cantor's was victimized by the British tools on the
continent, just as British agent Niels Bohr played a
prominent role in that filthy business during the present
century . . . as a shocked Werner Heisenberg notes in
respect to Bohr's atrocious antics toward Schroedinger.

Einstein, although predominantly a protege and
prisoner of the British, had enough independence of
character both to be shocked and to plainly discredit one of
the architects of this evil, Bertrand Russell, in print,
echoing similar views by the neo-Kantian Ernst Cassirer.

Yet, although the British inner circles have known
that they have been perpetrating knowingly monstrous
frauds and crimes, in general they have also mystified
themselves with respect to reason and scientific method.
Newton's preoccupation with the most infantile sort of
black magic, and his involvement in one of the nasty black
religious cults developed within Royal Society circles, his
insanity during the 1690s, involve the desperation of the
members of the Royal Society on account of their inability
to command the sort of creative powers manifest in those
from whom they plagiarized and whom they defamed. It
was the same with the wretched Aristotle.

The ruling British elite are like animals--not only in
their morality, but in their outlook on knowledge. They are
clever animals, who are masters of the wicked nature of
their own species, and recognize ferally the distinctions of

the hated human species.   Nonetheless, obsessively dedicated to being such animals, they can not assimilate those qualities unique to true human beings.

THE PHYSICS OF THE MATTER

The "n" and "n+1" orderings of continua arise not only in the comparison of entropic doctrines of physics and chemistry with respect to living processes. They occur in the experimental domain of physics itself.   They arise there in a twofold way: through the crucial fallacies intrinsic to accredited physics doctrines, and in certain key aspects of the experimental realm.   Not accidentally, the two aspects often intersect: an "anomalous" experimental phenomenon often corresponds to the problem of an intrinsic fallacy of accredited physics.

The general problem has been outlined by Uwe Parpart[9] and matters of detail have been covered by a number of articles reported either in the journals of the Fusion Energy Foundation or by the science staff of U.S. Labor Party intelligence.[10]   The problem of the electron[11] and the related problem of negentropic types of anomalous phenomena in plasma regimes locate the problem.

In certain types of phenomena occurring in plasma regimes, the process initially determined ostensibly according to ordinary, accredited physics doctrines, is transformed to produce self-sustaining or even reproductive phenomena, such as the vortices occurring in plasma-focus experiments for solitons.   The latter phenomena "violate" the basic laws of physics as ordinarily defined, to the effect that the causal features of the process are subject to accountability, but the consequences of this causal connection are not determinable in terms of the initial conditions from which starting-point they are produced.

This intersects the fact that an electron-particle could not exist, according to prevailing doctrines of existing physics, if it were a particle, and yet in many respects it behaves as if it were a particle. The crux of the difficulty is that the available gravitational forces to hold the particle together as a particle are miniscule with respect to the electromagnetic forces driving it apart.[12]

However. it has been shown that so-called elementary particles and negentropic sorts of plasma anomalies, such as vortices and solitons, are distinguished inclusively by the same Schroedinger-De Broglie properties. This indicates that the electron may be likened, at least conceptually, to the vortices in a plasma-focus experiment. In that case, the existence of the particle-form involves none of the paradoxes cited.

Therefore. we have a case of the "n continuum" being transformed into an "n+l continuum." Moreover, the "n +1 continuum" for this case coincides on crucial points with the relevant biochemical evidence concerning the physics of living processes. If one discards the notion of chemical bonds associated with the paradoxical definition of the electron as a particle, and so forth, then chemical bonds must be reconceptualized accordingly. The altered conceptions indicated as appropriate are much improved in the sense of being more agreeable to the crucial biological evidence. Whether living processes are in the same "n+1 continuum" as the negentropic singularities of experimental physics is an open issue; perhaps we must go from an "n+1" to "n+2" to arrive at living processes.

What is conclusively illustrated by that sort of evidence (it is also demonstrated in other ways) is that the scalar notion of energy and of the characteristics of "n" continua traditional to modern physics, are useful but ultimately false. Insofar as we can treat the "n continuum" experimentally as if it were a continuum *in those terms of conceptual reference*--keeping away, in particular, from the singularities of the "very small" and the paradoxes of the "very large," the scalar notion of energy and the constant speed of light are ostensibly adequate, experimental conceptions of physics. However, breaking outside those limiting circumstances for experimental investigation, or attempting to complete the conceptual apparatus of physics for the universe in terms of the mathematical physics of the "n continuum," science falls into contradictions and absurdities. This should cause no panic. Quite the contrary. All this is as we should have suspected. Science does not thus become less accessible to reason; it warns us that we must proceed now in accordance with what reason should have informed us beforehand.

The ostensible characteristic of a sub-continuum is a characteristic of that continuum in a conditional sense, but also merely a simplified aspect of the actual characteristic. The actual characteristic must be at the same time the characteristic of the universe described by the going over from an "n" into "n+1" into "n+2" and so forth continua, each continuum of which process is necessarily efficient with respect to its "predecessors." This characteristic is the transfinite for which the ostensible characteristics of each sub-continuum are enumerable predicates. Furthermore, this *transinvariant* cannot be linearizable, is not a constant, but is a constant principle of self development, of true negentropy.

Abelard might, were he alive, put it this way, God, the prime existence, is a creative principle which creates universes as the instruments for mediating the process of continued creation to ever higher states. Ibn Sina (Avicenna) has already defined this principle as the "necessary existent." Nicholas of Cusa defined it rigorously to the same effect as the "Non-Other."

Werner Heisenberg, among others, could not have erred as he did (in his adoption of the Copenhagen doctrine and postulating his notion of "indeterminacy") if he had grasped the epistemological significance of Max Planck's quantum-of-action. What Planck demonstrated, in effect, was that in the "very small" one encountered not some ultimate irreducible particle, but a *singularity*. The work of Schroedinger and De Broglie precisely intersected and advanced upon that feature of Planck's contribution. The cited paradox of the electron's existence as a supposed particle intersects Planck, Schroedinger, De Broglie et al. to the same effect. Indeed, during the middle 1950s De Broglie anticipated the existence of  such phenomena as solitons and plasma vortices on related grounds.[13] If Heisenberg had been qualified in epistemology, rather than conditioned to the sort of neo-

Kantian outlook he has reported and outlined, he should have recognized that Riemann had already fully anticipated the necessary nature of physics to such purposes, and should have recognized, further, that this entire problem was already posed by Leibniz's criticism of Descartes on "inertia," and otherwise anticipated in the broadest sense by Plato's Ionian and allied predecessors.

We focus on this point in two ways. First, we summarize the significance of the electron. Second, the connection between philosophy and physics.

The electron (and other "elementary'" particles), being an existence determined in the "n+1 continuum," is efficient with respect to the "n continuum," but is not determinable as an existence within the latter. It is, therefore, a *singularity* within the latter. This state of affairs becomes paradoxical only if one clings to the mistaken notion that the scalar determination of energy, in an "n continuum" characterized by a constant speed of light is an adequate representation of the universe. As long as that delusion is gripped, then the existence of the electron becomes a fact which threatens to demoralize science. Then, the doctrine of Heisenberg, or the more chaotic, despairing view of a von Weizacker tends to follow as a reflection of that demoralization. If the evidence of the electron's existence as a singularity is accepted, the opposite vantage-point, then the result is a mobilization of joyful efforts to discover the new, larger reality of the universe which has been proven available to us in this manner.

The problem of the well-tempered system is identical. Human beings are not vibrating rods, or anything else determinable according to the physics of an "n continuum." They are singularities of the "n+2" (for purposes of reference). They are efficient with respect to the n continuum. Their relations, insofar as they are mediated within the realm of the n continuum, have aspects which are partially determinable in terms of the physics of vibrating rods. However, music as *human music,* as the communication between the human singularities mediated in that way, is not determinable within the n continuum but only in the "n+2" continuum.

Physics can only progress as physics. It is the worst sort of absurdity to judge the fragments of Thales, Heraclitus, et al., from the standpoint of attempting to show how close or remote those minds were from the conceptions of modern physics. The issue of mind. fire (energy) and *continuous substance* (matter-field continuity) in Thales is not a matter of physics subcategories as such. It is a matter of *method.* It is a question of how the categorical questions concerning the lawful ordering of the universe shall be posed to consciousness *at the level of reason,* for the purpose of rigorously ordering the production of hypotheses bearing upon the principles of universal lawfulness.

This knowledge concerning categorical questions of that sort is not physics in the sense we use the term "physics" ordinarily. It is a distinction between those directions of hypothesis-making which are useful, and those other directions which are methodologically manifestly absurd.

One cannot spin out concrete physics from a philosopher's chair. The relationship of philosophy to physics is, more narrowly, to discern which philosophical statements by physicists are intrinsically, methodologically absurd. On the positive side, given adequate knowledge of physics to date, philosophy shows us how to select the experimental conception which will be most fruitful in gaining the next step of progress in mastery of the principles appropriate to physics. That, in general, is all that philosophy can accomplish with respect to positive sciences. That is all, but that is indispensable to the progress of science. That is the means by which the approach selected by the creative scientist is properly determined--just the *approach,* just the *indispensable* matter of approach.

The case of the electron paradox is appropriately illustrative. Confronted with a problem involving "elementary particle" experimentation, knowing that the electron doctrine of accredited physics is intrinsically absurd is representative of that kind of philosophical knowledge which guides the experimenter to the most fruitful experimental hypotheses. That illustrates the method to be applied in a more generalized way to order the progress of science in general.

Reason, which is definable in a consistent way in principle over the ages, is thus a kind of "constant." However, reason is not otherwise constant, not linearizable. As it assimilates to itself the fruits of its own accomplishments in mastering the lawful ordering of the universe, reason develops itself in its particular powers. *In this process of self development of reason*, mediated through the practical scientific progress effected by efficient action of reason, reason parallels and intersects the fundamental, *also self developing,* lawful ordering of the universe.

THE HIERARCHY OF SCIENTIFIC KNOWLEDGE

The discoveries in the domain of the physical sciences accomplished by the U.S. Labor Party and its collaborators, and reflected in part in this report, were accomplished in the manner indicated. Through assimilation of this method, as embodied for reference in the subject of political economy, recruits to the Labor Party and associated organizations were originally drawn from young persons representing the most promising minds of the late 1960s and early 1970s--and through their own individual and collaborative efforts in mastering physics, biology and so forth, some of these persons were able to produce original contributions to scientific progress in those fields. This represented, in some instances, important new discoveries by individuals or teams of individuals. In other instances, it represented the kind of discovery involved in appreciating the broader implications of the discoveries reported by others. Method, informed by existing scientific knowledge, acted, as the power of informed reason, to advance the body of knowledge by which it was informed.

Although those persons probably would have tended to succeed in their professions with distinction in any case, the overall quality of distinctions associated with the U.S. Labor Party's work has been added to their powers, directly or indirectly as a benefit contributed by this writer's work of the 1950s.

The kernel of this writer's distinctive, original contributions to human knowledge is the successful application, beginning in the early 1950s, of the cited Riemann and Cantor conceptions to solving the basic errors in Karl Marx's three-volume *Capital.* This effort was "energized" by a youthful adoption of the methodological outlook of Gottfried Leibniz--in which connection Leibniz's *Monadology* was outstanding. Any body of knowledge which erred from the standpoint of that methodological outlook was viewed as intrinsically in error, and the existence of such error became then a source of intellectual "tension," impelling the writer to reject the indicated doctrines as given, and, if the matter involved were important, to seek a remedy agreeable to appropriate method.

The fundamental error of Marx's *Capital,* for purposes of reference, is this. Although Marx's own Neoplatonic outlook led him to correct systematic conclusions concerning the essential "internal contradiction" of capitalist accumulation as a whole, in all Marx's efforts to develop a set of linear equations for "extended reproduction" from the set of linear equations for "simple reproduction," he failed--and necessarily so. "Simple reproduction" is an arbitrary, heuristic construct, an effort to imagine the simplest case in which a capitalist economy perpetuates itself on the same level of technology in the same extent. Marx attempted to move to the case of "extended reproduction," in first approximation, without considering the effects of technological progress, but only extension in scale (through investment of portions of surplus value in additional plant, equipment, materials, employment of productive labor, and so forth). Consequently, on this side of his efforts, Marx's work ends up in the wretched confusion typified by the material which Marx's editor, Friedrich Engels, assembled as the concluding chapter of *Capital*, Volume II. For related reasons, all efforts of Marxologists to explicate the "internal contradictions" of capitalist accumulation in terms of systems of equations for "extended reproduction" become increasingly absurd as the profession of convergence upon a solution within Marx's terms is more energetically advanced.

This is not the only political-economic error in Marx's work. As we have noted elsewhere, although the kernel of Marx's method was essentially a reconstitution of the Neoplatonic dialectical method of Leibniz et al., somewhat better informed in aspects than Leibniz, the elaboration of Marx's work was contained within his credulous acceptance of a prevailing historical mythology, essentially an acceptance of the British falsification of history. This infectious blunder affects many aspects of Marx's work. It affects his political-economic work in the respect that in his elaboration of the internal order of capitalist accumulation processes, he adopted the fictitious, British model of "industrial capitalist development" as the empirical case for which competent theory must account. This effort to adapt his elaboration of political-economic theory to the fictitious British model is the chief determinant of the major errors in Marx's work on that subject.

The results of this writer's work of the 1950s, which included an emphasis on the actuality of American industrial reality, a quality almost entirely lacking in Marx's work, led to a new, independent political economic theory, which in no way depended upon the presumed authority of elements of Marx's own work, although it benefited most substantially from knowledge of the work of Marx. This new economic theoretical method was crucially proven by testing of hypotheses against emerging developments of the 1950s and 1960s, establishing the newly developed theoretical economics as uniquely competent in contrast to all extant competing theories, Marx's included.[14]

The essential feature of this economic doctrine was that the principle of technological progress was the primary determinant of economic processes, rather than an "added-in" feature, as Marx's approach had attempted erroneously to deal with the matter.

This effort not only circumscribed the problems of method generally, but was associated with an intensive study of history, both history as such and archaeological history, to the purpose of discovering empirical indicators of the characteristics of precapitalist economies, and the characteristic philosophical outlooks of precapitalist societies. The results of this were coherently embodied in the instructional program on which the predecessor organization of the U.S. Labor Party was established as an organization *ex novo* (as opposed to an organization assembled from indoctrinated elements of previously existing organizations, etc.).

Over the years, the question often arose, what is the basis in authority for imposing certain criteria of hypothesis upon work in the physical sciences. To this question, the consistent answer given was, and rightly so, the proof of that method in political economy. *The fact that the order of the universe appropriate to the above-indicated features of the physics of Riemann has been crucially proven once in the domain of political economy proves also that the entire universe is ordered according to such principles.* Political economy, viewed and developed in that way, is the highest form of science, the crucial source of authority for scientific knowledge in all domains.

The crucial experiment upon which human knowledge is essentially dependent is human existence itself.[15] Since all particular knowledge is ultimately and necessarily superseded, no form of knowledge as such (understanding) can embody proof of the validity of scientific knowledge in a lasting way. What is proven by human existence is the efficiency of creative reason in ordering the progress of knowledge to the effect of maintaining and advancing the human species's ecological population-potential. It is as political economy situates the direct connection between progress of knowledge and changes in the ecological population-potential of human practice based on advancing knowledge, that the essential connection is made, and uniquely so. It could not be otherwise.

It is to Karl Marx's credit that he attempted to found his efforts on realizing that perception. His "Theses on Feuerbach" and the first section, "Feuerbach," of *The German Ideology,* are most notable to this effect. Also notable is the recurrence of that Neoplatonic notion as the conception of "Freedom-Necessity" in *Capital* III, Sec. 7. Marx's failure was broadly his effort to elaborate his work within British historical mythologies, and to close himself off from the "inner secrets" of the elite by his foolish "materialist" emphasis respecting the determination of ideas. Both these principal errors were necessarily interdependent.

HISTORIOGRAPHICAL METHOD

History is to be understood as the subjective connection between "objective" events and conditions perceived, as they are "subjectively" perceived, and the "objective" consequences of the human actions (or acts of omission) taken in consequence of such perception. The crucial subject matter is not merely that "subjective" element itself, but the processes which determine the character and development of that "subjective" element.

The accomplished historian must be both a person who has mastered that approach in essentials, and also a person who has progressed further, to the competence to adduce the "subjective" element of history from the patterns of "objective" behavior which the "subjective" element has left as its spoor.

The case of the militia illustrates the problems of the latter work.

Putting the case of the Roman republic to one side for a moment, the most effective form of warfare is the mobilization of the resources of a state in the form of a well-trained militia. This depends, in turn, upon the constitution of the state in such forms that the general population can be "trusted" by the rulers as the *armed population*--trained in arms, with arms in hand when called.

An oppressing ruler dare not persist in this practice, but prefers either special armed bodies of volunteer professionals or mercenary forces. His military policy centers as much on subjugating the population as contending against foreign adversaries.

The case is not cut and dried. There are exceptions of importance, and of some frequency of recurrence. Even so, the uses of the militia versus more limited or mercenary armed forces have clear, if partial implications concerning the political character of the state and the mentality of the states. The case of the mercenary force is virtually conclusive.

Rome has a double implication.

The fact that the affairs of the Roman republic were ordered from an early time, according to available knowledge, by the cult of Apollo, is of utmost importance in showing that accredited historiography on this subject is grossly flawed. The character of evolving Roman law, also consistent with the antihumanist doctrines of politics and law of the Peripatetics, is also relevant. Rome's successes, including its conquests of its Italian and Etruscan neighbors, have a different moral quality than Roman writers and their admirers would have us believe.

Insanity glorified: During the British push to revive the tradition of nominalist Roman law in the 18th century, monetarist propagandists used Apollonian images to promote the worst aspects of classical tradition. Jacques Louis David's "Oath of the Horatii" [1785] [above] depicts with "nobility" three fanatic Roman brothers who stoically vowed to "win or die for liberty" in individual combat--while their wives sit stoically anguished on the side. In a similar vein, his "Battle of the Romans and the Sabines" [1799] [facing page]--in which the Roman Sabine wives hurl themselves and their children between the Roman and Sabine armies in an effort to stop the conflict--glorifies one of the more insane episodes of Roman mythology. The psychological insight of Rembrandt's "Oath of Julius Civilis" provides an instructive comparison with the Apollonianism of David's Horatii.

Nonetheless, the Roman policy of the militia was an integral feature of Roman successes overall. At the point that Roman moral and economic decay progressed to the point the militia basis evaporated, beginning the point that Rome could no longer feed itself except by looting foreign nations, the Roman Empire was doomed.

Let there be no foolish assumption that perhaps this report exaggerates the folly of most existing appreciations of the history of the Roman republic. According to Livy and other sources, it was the cult of Apollo which governed Roman policy with the same sorts of tricks the cult employed during other regions at that period. Moreover, it is repeatedly noted that the loot taken in war was shared generously with the cult of Apollo. The role of the cult of Apollo in bringing the Roman legions to Greece, the cult's sponsorship of Julius Caesar of the Marian faction, using he methods of the Phrygian cult of Dionysus, and the Stoic cult are also indicative. Rome was not some out-of-the-way development of the republican period, but during much of that period, at least, was a part of the relatively global apparatus being deployed by the cult at Delphi and by way of Ptolemaic Egypt.

The evidence of technological and scientific progress is another crucial objective fact of archeology. The existence of a flourishing city-state of large population is already an indication of the city-builders' faction and outlook. The rate of progress, and the quality of existence of various strata of the population, as well as their occupations, is similarly indicative.

The primary distinction to be made is whether the state was dominated by city-builders' forces, the oligarchical faction, or by a struggle between the two forces. Objective features of the archaeological evidence, especially those bearing on rates and directions of developments, are crucial. These indications inform us, to a corresponding degree of accuracy, of the mentality of the leading forces of that state. We can presently correlate literary and archaeological records adequately back to the eighth century BC to be able to go back at least two millennia earlier with principally archaeological evidence in hand, to "reconstruct" essential features of the "subjective" element--the element decisive to historiography.

We know, both from history and modern experience, how the two primary opposing policies are determined. The Hobbesian view and its correlatives are associated with the rule of heteronomic impulses, which tend to be strengthened by "entropic" developments in culture and political-economy. The humanist outlook is always originated through great intellects, an influential political and scientific intelligentsia, in whole sweeps of cultural progress usually associated with the most prominent influence of a single creative mind. These humanist influences become hegemonic through successful technological progress, which creates the conditions under which the ordinary individual of urban-centered culture values others and himself or herself in terms of the practical importance society attributes to the increased power of individuals for discovery, transmission and applications of technological and related advances in knowledge.

What defeats the human race repeatedly is "practical politics." The adaptation of policies of factions to prevailing mythologies and prejudices creates advantages for the enemies of humanity, because human progress occurs only through the hubristic intellectual leadership and action of a political intelligentsia--an elite!-- to effects which are feasible but nonetheless contrary to traditional practice and prevailing prejudices concerning "practicality."

The history of man and of ideas is not determined by objective circumstances as such, but subjectively, by the action of creative powers of reason, informed by existing knowledge and with means available, to transform the objective domain according to directions specified by creative reason. Objective circumstances determine the potentialities of specific actions (and associated kinds of ideas) which reason may employ.

The history of mankind, those circumstantial aspects understood, is the history of reason's struggle against the oligarchical principle of unreason. Not to be a Neoplatonic humanist today is to be morally not a member of the human species.

Notes

1. Allen Salisbury.

2. Cf. Dr. Richard Pollak, "Evolution--Beyond Darwin and Mendel," *Fusion Energy Foundation Newsletter*, Vol. II, No. 4 (May 1977), pp. 42-53.

3. Cf. Dr. Ned Rosinsky, "Drosophila Embryology--The Dynamics of Evolution," *Fusion Energy Foundation Newsletter*, Vol. II, No. 4 (May 1977), pp. 54-59.

4. Bertrand Russell, notably, threw himself into a sort of psychedelic literary fit on this point.

5. Criton Zoakos has employed Greek-language sources to the effect of more than corroborating this writer's established judgment concerning the Ionians.

6. The research and related work on this matter has been developed in part by Anno Hellenbroich and others, and by a New York-centered group of collaborators including Dr. Peter Wyer, Vivian Freyre, Katharine Burdman. On Bacon and Bull, see P. Wyer and M. Stahlman, "Rock Music and the Mass Marketing of Terrorism," *New Solidarity*, Vol. VIII, No. 85 (Dec. 30, 1977). See also, Anno Hellenbroich, "Think Like Beethoven," *The Campaigner*, Vol. XI, No. 1, (February 1978), pp. 46-61; and K. Burdman, "The

Case of J.S. Bach," *New Solidarity*, Vol. VIII, No. 75 (Nov. 18, 1977).

7. Felix Mendelssohn is usually credited, wrongly, with "resurrecting" Bach's music. Rather, the British elected to abandon their near-century efforts to suppress Bach through Mendelssohn's resurrecting the "simpler" Bach as part of his effort to direct music toward romanticism, away from the "complicated" music of Beethoven. Wagner's contribution to this wickedness was his effort to edit features of Beethoven's works and to poison the musicological doctrine respecting their performance. Both were working for the antihumanist Black Guelph networks, and doing so as a matter of political consciousness.

8. Cf. Carol White, *Energy Potential* (New York: Campaigner Publications, Inc., 1978), passim.

9. Uwe Parpart, "The Concept of the Transfinite," *The Campaigner*, Vol. IX, Nos. 1-2, (January-February 1976), pp. 6-66.

10. Cf. Dr. Steven Bardwell's series on the implications of nonlinear processes in controlled plasmas: "Fusion Plasma, An Overview of the Research," *Fusion Energy Foundation Newsletter*, Vol. II, No. 1 (July-August 1976), pp. 21-23; "The History of the Theory and Observation of Ordered Phenomena in Magnetized Plasmas," *FEF Newsletter*, Vol. II, No. 2 (September 1976), pp. 19-31; "The Implications of Nonlinearity," *FEF Newsletter*, Vol. II, No. 3 (March 1977), pp. 4-16; "Geometry and Causality," *Fusion*, Vol. I, No. 7 (June 1978). See also Dr. Morris Levitt, "Linearity and

Entropy: Ludwig Boltzmann and the Second Law of Thermodynamics," *FEF Newsletter,* Vol. II. No. 2 (September 1976). pp. 3-18.

11. The problem was developed primarily by Dr. W. Bostick, in the form it was attacked by him and also by members of the U.S. Labor Party's science staff. Cf. Dr. Winston H. Bostick, "The Pinch Effect Revisited," *International Journal of Fusion Energy*, Vol. I, No. 1 (March 1977).

12. Bostick et al. proposed the effort to apply the lessons of plasma-vortex physics to the electron, etc.

13. Louis De Broglie, *Une tentative d'interpretation causale et non lineaire de la mecanique ondulatoire,* (Paris: Gauthier Villars, 1956), chapter 18. This information was communicated to Uwe Parpart by Georges Lochak, director of La Fondation Louis De Broglie in Paris.

14. Lyn Marcus (Lyndon H. LaRouche, Jr.), *Dialectical Economics* (Lexington, Mass: D.C. Heath, 1975). This textbook embodies the lectures given as a one-semester course beginning Spring 1966, at various locations.

15. This point is embodied as the kernel-conception of Karl Marx's accomplishments. Cf. *The German Ideology,* §l: "Feuerbach."

Made in the USA
Lexington, KY
01 August 2018